D1530646

Writing

DISCOVERING CAREERS

Writing

Ferguson's
An Infobase Learning Company

Discovering Careers: Writing

Ferguson's
An imprint of Infobase Learning
132 West 31st Street
New York NY 10001

Library of Congress Cataloging-in-Publication Data
Writing. — 1st ed.
     p. cm. — (Discovering careers)
Includes bibliographical references and index.
ISBN-13: 978-0-8160-8060-1 (hardcover : alk. paper)
ISBN-10: 0-8160-8060-7 (hardcover : alk. paper) 1. Authorship—Vocational guid-ance—Juvenile literature. 2. Editing—Vocational guidance—Juvenile literature. I. Ferguson Publishing.
PN153.W65 2012
808'.02023—dc23   2011025161

Ferguson's books are available at special discounts when purchased in bulk quantities for businesses, associations, institutions, or sales promotions. Please call our Special Sales Department in New York at (212) 967-8800 or (800) 322-8755.

You can find Ferguson's on the World Wide Web at
http://www.infobaselearning.com

Text design by Erik Lindstrom and Erika K. Arroyo
Composition by Erika K. Arroyo
Cover printed by Yurchak Printing, Landisville, Pa.
Book printed and bound by Yurchak Printing, Landisville, Pa.

Printed in the United States of America

This book is printed on acid-free paper.

CONTENTS

Introduction

You may not have decided yet what you want to be in the future. And you don't have to decide right away. You do know that right now you are interested in writing. Do any of the statements below describe you? If so, you may want to begin thinking about what a career as a writer might mean for you.

_____ I love writing.

_____ I enjoy reading books, magazines, newspapers, and articles on the Internet.

_____ I am good at conducting research.

_____ I enjoy writing stories about trips I've taken with my parents.

_____ I like to write plays.

_____ I am good at giving speeches and oral presentations.

_____ I love watching movies and plays. I like to write short reviews about them for friends and family.

_____ I have my own blog on the Internet.

_____ I write for the school paper or literary magazine.

_____ I like writing about my favorite sports team.

_____ I enjoy revising and editing school papers.

_____ I like to share my opinions with others.

_____ My favorite class is English.

_____ I am good at teaching others about proper grammar, punctuation, and spelling.

_____ I like writing short stories.

_____ I love music and writing songs.

Discovering Careers: Writing is a book about writing careers, from columnists, to fashion writers, to reporters. Writers express their ideas or report facts in words for books, magazines, newspapers, advertisements, radio, television, and the Internet. They are very creative and have excellent research skills.

This book describes many possibilities for future careers in writing. Read through it and see how the different careers are connected. For example, if you are interested in journalism, you will want to read the chapters on Columnists, Editors, Reporters and Correspondents, Sportswriters, and other careers. If you are interested in music, you will want to read the chapter on Songwriters. If you want to work in the movie industry, you should read the articles on Movie Writers and Critics, and Screenwriters. If you want to become a teacher, you should read the article on Writing Teachers. Perhaps you want to work in the advertising industry. If so, then you should read the article on Copywriters. Go ahead and explore!

What Do Writers Do?

The first section of each chapter begins with a heading such as "What Environmental Writers Do" or "What Technical Writers Do." It tells what it's like to work at this job. It describes typical responsibilities and assignments. You will find out about working conditions. Which writers work in newsrooms? Which ones work in offices? Which ones travel to restaurants, national parks, movie sets, or to vacation spots to do their jobs? This section answers all these questions.

How Do I Become a Writer?

The section called "Education and Training" tells you what schooling you need for employment in each job—a high school diploma, training at a junior college, a college degree, or more. It also talks about on-the-job training that you could expect to receive after you're hired.

How Much Do Writers Earn?

The "Earnings" section gives the average salary figures for the job described in the chapter. These figures give you a general idea of how much money people with this job can make. Keep in mind that many people really earn more or less than the amounts given here because actual salaries depend on many different things, such as the talent and skill level of the writer, the size of the organization, the location of the organization, and the amount of education, training, and experience you have. Generally, but not always, bigger companies or organizations located in major cities pay more than smaller ones in smaller cities and towns, and people with more skill, education, training, and experience earn more. Also remember that these figures are current averages. They will probably be different by the time you are ready to enter the workforce.

What Will the Future Be Like for Writers?

The "Outlook" section discusses the employment outlook for the career: whether the total number of people employed in this career will increase or decrease in the coming years and whether jobs in this field will be easy or hard to find. These predictions are based on economic conditions, the size and makeup of the population, interest in the particular area of writing, and other factors. They come from the U.S. Department of Labor, professional associations, and other sources.

Keep in mind that these predictions are general statements. No one knows for sure what the future will be like. Also remember that the employment outlook is a general statement about an industry and does not necessarily apply to everyone. A determined and talented person may be able to find a job in an industry or career with the worst outlook. And a person without ambition and the proper training will find it difficult to find a job in even a booming industry or career field.

Where Can I Find More Information?

Each chapter includes a sidebar called "For More Info." It lists resources that you can contact to find out more about the field and careers in the field. You will find names, addresses, phone numbers, e-mail addresses, and Web sites of writing-oriented associations and organizations.

Extras

Every chapter has a few extras. There are photos that show writers in action. There are sidebars and notes on ways to explore the field, fun facts, profiles of people in the field, and lists of Web sites and books that might be helpful. At the end of the book you will find three additional sections: "Glossary," "Browse and Learn More," and "Index." The Glossary gives brief definitions of words that relate to education, career training, or employment that you may be unfamiliar with. The Browse and Learn More section lists writing-related books, periodicals, and Web sites to explore. The Index includes all the job titles mentioned in the book.

It's not too soon to think about your future. We hope you discover several possible career choices. Happy hunting!

Columnists

What Columnists Do

Columnists write their opinions for newspapers, magazines, and Web sites. Some columnists write about personal experience. Others write about current events.

Columns are written on a schedule, perhaps every day, week, or month, depending on how often the newspaper or magazine comes out. Like other journalists, columnists must complete their work by strict deadlines.

Columnists sometimes specialize in one area. Some may write humor columns, while others write in a more serious tone about government and politics, health, or business.

Coming up with new ideas is one of the hardest parts of being a columnist. Columnists search through newspapers, magazines, and the Internet for ideas. They also talk to people in the community and read e-mail and mail they receive from readers. Next, they conduct research to gather facts to support their viewpoints. Finally, they write their columns, usually using a computer.

Most columnists work in newsrooms or magazine offices. But some work out of their homes or private offices.

Most columnists start out as reporters first. After they gain experience, they may be offered a job as a columnist.

Columns are different than regular news stories because they usually take a side on an issue. A columnist must have strong opinions. They must clearly explain facts and observations that support their opinions. They must not be afraid when people disagree or challenge their ideas. Other important traits

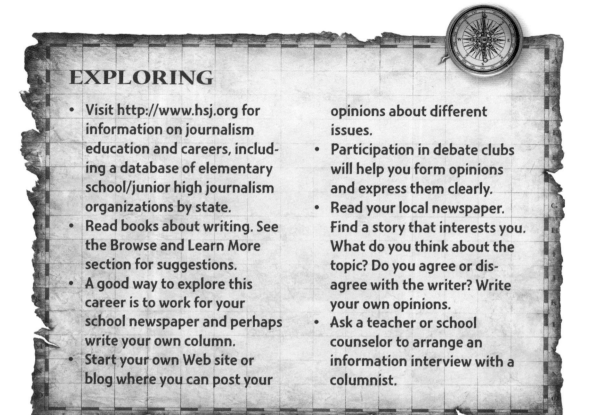

EXPLORING

- Visit http://www.hsj.org for information on journalism education and careers, including a database of elementary school/junior high journalism organizations by state.
- Read books about writing. See the Browse and Learn More section for suggestions.
- A good way to explore this career is to work for your school newspaper and perhaps write your own column.
- Start your own Web site or blog where you can post your opinions about different issues.
- Participation in debate clubs will help you form opinions and express them clearly.
- Read your local newspaper. Find a story that interests you. What do you think about the topic? Do you agree or disagree with the writer? Write your own opinions.
- Ask a teacher or school counselor to arrange an information interview with a columnist.

for columnists include being able to produce work under deadline pressure, having excellent interviewing skills, and the ability to use computers and the Internet.

Almost every newspaper runs some type of column. Newspapers employ their own columnists or publish columns they buy from syndicates (companies that sell published material to several newspapers at once) or both.

Education and Training

Reading and writing are important subjects for future columnists. In high school you should take English, journalism, social studies, speech, computer science, and typing. It is a good idea to try to write for your yearbook or school newspaper.

After high school, you must go to a university and earn at least a bachelor's degree. Most editors prefer that their employees hold a degree in journalism. Others prefer applicants with a bachelor's in liberal arts and a master's in journalism.

Much of your training will come on the job as a reporter. Reporters learn the key parts of being a columnist: interviewing, research, and people skills. Also, reporters learn how to manage their time, write quickly and to the point, and finish before deadline.

DID YOU KNOW?

Where Columnists Work

- Internet media companies
- Magazines
- Newspapers
- Self-employment

Earnings

The U.S. Department of Labor classifies columnists with reporters and correspondents, although columnists usually make higher salaries than reporters. The median annual income for reporters was $34,530 in 2010. Those just starting out in the field and those employed by small newspapers and magazines

Profile: Art Buchwald (1925–2007)

Art Buchwald was a U.S. journalist who became famous for his political columns. He won a Pulitzer Prize in 1982 for his comments on political figures.

Buchwald was born in Mount Vernon, New York. He attended the University of Southern California from 1945 to 1948. Then he went to Paris, where he began to write a humorous column on life in Europe. He moved to Washington, D.C., in 1962.

Buchwald wrote 34 books. *Laid Back in Washington* (1982) is a collection of his newspaper columns. *Leaving Home: A Memoir* was published in 1994. Other works include *Art Buchwald's Paris* (1954), *I Chose Capitol Punishment* (1963), and *I Never Danced at the White House* (1973).

FOR MORE INFO

For a list of accredited programs in journalism and mass communications, visit the ACEJMC Web site.
Accrediting Council on Education in Journalism and Mass Communications (ACEJMC)
University of Kansas School of Journalism and Mass Communications
Stauffer-Flint Hall, 1435 Jayhawk Boulevard
Lawrence, KS 66045-7575
785-864-3973
http://www2.ku.edu/~acejmc

For information on careers in journalism, contact
American Society of Journalists and Authors
1501 Broadway, Suite 403
New York, NY 10036-5505
212-997-0947
http://www.asja.org

This association provides general educational information on all areas of journalism, including newspapers, magazines, television, radio, and the Internet.
Association for Education in Journalism and Mass Communication
234 Outlet Pointe Boulevard, Suite A
Columbia, SC 29210-5667
803-798-0271
http://www.aejmc.com

To read *The Journalist's Road to Success: A Career Guide,* visit the DJNF Web site.

Dow Jones News Fund (DJNF)
PO Box 300
Princeton, NJ 08543-0300
609-452-2820
djnf@dowjones.com
https://www.newsfund.org

For information on a career as a newspaper columnist, contact
National Society of Newspaper Columnists
PO Box 411532
San Francisco, CA 94141-1532
415-488-6762
http://www.columnists.com

For information about working as a writer and union membership, contact
National Writers Union
256 West 38th Street, Suite 703
New York, NY 10018-9807
212-254-0279
nwu@nwu.org
http://www.nwu.org

For a variety of journalism resources, visit the SPJ Web site.
Society of Professional Journalists (SPJ)
Eugene S. Pulliam National Journalism Center
3909 North Meridian Street
Indianapolis, IN 46208-4011
317-927-8000
http://www.spj.org

earned less than $20,000. Experienced columnists earned salaries of $75,000 or more.

Outlook

It is likely that the number of columnists, small to begin with, will remain constant. There will be strong competition for these jobs. The best place to start is at smaller publications, where newspaper reporters and magazine editorial assistants take on many tasks, but they also get promoted faster. However, the pay is less than at bigger publications. The Internet is providing columnists with many new opportunities. But many of these positions offer little or no pay and do not provide full-time work.

Copywriters

What Copywriters Do

Copywriters write the words of advertisements, including the written text in print ads and on the Internet. They also write the words that are spoken in radio and television ads, which are also called spots. Their main goal is to convince the public to choose or favor certain goods, services, and personalities. Most copywriters work in the advertising industry.

Copywriters may have to come up with their own idea and words for an ad, but generally the client's account manager and head designer generate the idea. Once the idea behind the ad is presented, copywriters begin gathering as much information as possible about the client through library research, interviews, the Internet, observation, and other methods. They study advertising trends and review surveys of consumer preferences (what people like in a product or service). They keep detailed notes from which they will draw material for the ad. Once their research has been organized, copywriters begin working on the written parts of the ad. They may have a standard theme or "pitch" to work with that has been developed in previous ads. One such example, using what is called a tagline, is seen in the popular milk campaigns promoting its health benefits and other advantages—beauty, athleticism, and intelligence. ("Milk: It does a body good.")

The process of developing copy is exciting, although it can also involve detailed and solitary work. After researching one idea, a writer might discover that a different approach or related topic would better reach consumers.

EXPLORING

- Read books about writing. See the Browse and Learn More section for some suggestions.
- Read and listen to all sorts of advertisements. This will expose you to both good and bad writing styles and techniques and help you to identify why one approach works better than another.
- Try writing advertising copy that convinces someone to buy a product such as an iPod, a brand of cereal, or a new car.
- Take writing courses and workshops offered by your school or your local community to sharpen your writing skills.
- Tour local advertising firms, newspapers, publishers, or radio and television stations and interview some of the writers who work there.

When working on assignment, copywriters submit their ad drafts to their editor or the advertising account executive for approval. Writers often work through several drafts. They write and rewrite sections of the material as they proceed, searching for just the right way to promote the product, service, or other client need.

Copywriters may also write articles, bulletins, news releases, sales letters, speeches, and other related informative and promotional material. In addition to working in advertising, some copywriters work for public relations firms or in communications departments of large companies. Others work for government agencies.

Education and Training

If you are interested in becoming a copywriter, take high school courses in English, literature, foreign languages, business,

Tips for Success

To be a successful copywriter, you should

- be creative and able to express ideas clearly
- have strong communication skills—both written and oral
- be good at conducting research
- know how to use computers and the Internet
- be curious, persistent, and resourceful
- be able to accept constructive criticism of your work
- have the ability to work under pressure and tight deadlines

computer science, and typing. Work on your school newspaper, yearbook, or literary magazine to gain writing experience.

You will need to earn a college degree to be eligible for most copywriting positions. Many employers prefer that you have a broad liberal arts background or a major in English, literature, history, philosophy, or one of the social sciences. Other employers desire communications or journalism training in college. A number of schools offer courses in copywriting and other business writing.

Earnings

The U.S. Department of Labor reports that writers (including copywriters) who were employed in advertising and related services had mean annual earnings of $73,710 in 2010. Salaries for all writers ranged from less than $29,000 to $109,000 or more annually.

DID YOU KNOW?

There are approximately 50,100 advertising and public relations firms nationwide, employing more than 462,000 workers.

Source: U.S. Department of Labor

Outlook

Employment in the advertising industry—the main employer of copywriters—is only expected to be fair during the next decade. People entering this field should realize that the competition for jobs is extremely keen. The appeal of writing and advertising jobs will continue to grow. Many young graduates find the industry glamorous and exciting.

FOR MORE INFO

For profiles of advertising workers, career information, and a list of educational programs, contact
Advertising Educational Foundation
220 East 42nd Street, Suite 3300
New York, NY 10017-5806
212-986-8060
http://www.aef.com

For more information on the advertising industry, contact
American Advertising Federation
1101 Vermont Avenue, NW, Suite 500
Washington, DC 20005-3521
800-999-2231
aaf@aaf.org
http://www.aaf.org

For information on advertising agencies, contact
American Association of Advertising Agencies
405 Lexington Avenue, 18th Floor
New York, NY 10174-1801
212-682-2500
http://www.aaaa.org

For information about working as a writer and union membership, contact
National Writers Union
256 West 38th Street, Suite 703
New York, NY 10018-9807
212-254-0279
nwu@nwu.org
http://www.nwu.org

One important trend that will affect the employment of copywriters is specialization. Many agencies are increasing their focus on niche, or specialty, advertising. Expected high-growth areas include foreign-language programming, advertising aimed at specific ethnic groups, advertising targeted at the over-50 market, special events advertising and marketing, and direct marketing campaigns for retailers and technology companies. Copywriters who can offer skills such as the ability to write copy in a foreign language will be in demand.

In addition, the explosion of online advertising has created many new jobs, and companies are responding by placing advertising on the Web and creating Web sites that allow customers the ease and convenience of online shopping. All of these goods and services require copywriters to write ads that will promote and sell.

Editors

What Editors Do

When you read a book, magazine, newspaper, online text, or any other publication, you can thank *editors* for making the text easy to read and understand, grammatically correct, and otherwise well-written. In short, editors take the work of writers and prepare it for publication. They also assign topics to writers and supervise the articles through publication. Some editors write editorials to mold and stimulate public opinion. Editors often write, but they more often rewrite or revise the work of others. Editors have the authority to hire and fire writers. They also negotiate contracts and plan budgets.

Editors work for a variety of employers—virtually any company or organization that hires writers to write articles, books, advertising copy, or other text. Some major employers of editors include newspapers, magazines, book publishers, advertising agencies, public relations firms, corporations, nonprofit organizations, government agencies, and Internet companies. Some editors are self-employed and sell their services on a part-time basis to these companies and organizations.

At a small organization or publication, a single editor may be responsible for all the editorial duties. At large organizations, there are many specialized editors. A *senior* or *executive editor* supervises the work of *associate editors*, who are in charge of specific projects or specialty areas. For example, a fashion magazine may have a beauty editor, features editor, or main story editor, and photo editor. Each editor is responsible for obtaining, proofreading, rewriting, and sometimes writing

EXPLORING

- Visit http://www.hsj.org for information on journalism education and careers, including a database of elementary school/junior high journalism organizations by state.
- Work on a school newspaper or other publication. Your school may have a literary magazine. Or you can start a magazine for your class or school.

- Keep a journal. Write something every day. Write about anything that you find interesting. Practice writing short stories, poetry, or essays. Try to rework your writing until it is as good as you can make it.
- Make it a habit to read all kinds of publications—in print and online.
- Talk to an editor about his or her career.

articles. *Managing editors* supervise editors and other editorial staff. They coordinate production schedules, plan long-term publishing goals, and have many other responsibilities.

There are many other types of editors. *Acquisitions editors* find new writers and new projects. They find new ideas for books or magazines that will sell well. They find writers who can create the books or articles. Sometimes they assign a series of books or articles to one author. Acquisitions editors make sure authors turn in their manuscripts on time. They usually work with several authors at a time.

Production editors work with artists to design book and magazine covers and the interior pages, or for a layout that will be used online. They work with illustrators and photographers to create artwork for the publication or the Internet. They manage the page or electronic layout process. They make sure all

A newspaper editor looks over a page one mock-up of the following day's edition. (Elaine Thompson, AP Photo)

the parts of the book get to the printer on time or are posted online on schedule.

Copy editors help polish the author's writing. They review each page and make all the changes required to give the publication a good writing style. *Line editors* review the text to make sure specific style rules are obeyed. They make sure the same spelling is used for words where more than one spelling is correct (for example, grey and gray).

Photo editors are responsible for the look of final photographs to be published in a book or periodical or that are posted on the Internet. Some photo editors also work with video that is posted online. Photo editors are also known as *picture editors* and *multimedia editors*.

Proofreaders read the manuscript to make sure everything is spelled correctly and there are no errors in punctuation or grammar. *Fact checkers* make sure that all the facts in the text have been checked. They may check by contacting experts or the people quoted, or they may look in other publications to see if the information has been printed before.

Television and radio editors prepare news copy for broadcast by anchors and reporters.

Tips for Success

To be a successful editor, you should

- have excellent editing and writing skills
- be able to make quick decisions
- be able to meet deadlines
- enjoy supervising and teaching others
- be detail oriented
- have good research skills
- be able to focus for long periods of time
- be skilled at using computers, the Internet, multimedia, and social media

Education and Training

To prepare for a career as an editor, you should take high school courses in history, English, literature, journalism, social science, and typing.

A college degree is required for a career as an editor. Some employers look for a broad liberal arts background, but most prefer to hire people with degrees in English, communications, or journalism. A degree or class work in the specific subject of a special-interest publication—chemistry for a chemistry magazine—is also helpful.

Most editors do not begin their careers as editors, but rise through the ranks. They often are hired as proofreaders, fact checkers, or editorial assistants. Then they are promoted to assistant editor before they become editors. It is helpful to have

Questions Editors Ask

When editors read articles for the first time, they ask themselves questions like the following:

- Is the topic well defined and focused?
- Does the article contain facts, arguments, and explanations? If there are opinions, are the opinions well supported?
- Are the facts and ideas organized in a logical order?
- Are the introduction and conclusion interesting and effective?
- Has the writer given all the facts and answered all the questions a reader might ask?
- Is the article interesting to read?
- Are words spelled correctly? Is the grammar and punctuation correct?

writing experience, because so much of an editor's job is supervising the work of writers.

Earnings

Editors earned average salaries of $51,470 in 2010, according to the U.S. Department of Labor. Those just starting out in the field earned less than $29,000. Very experienced editors made more than $96,000. Newspaper, book, and periodical editors earned mean salaries of $58,270.

Outlook

Little employment change is expected for editors. There should continue to be jobs, but competition for the best positions will be very strong. Editors with advanced degrees and experience working with electronic publications and multimedia resources will have the best job prospects.

FOR MORE INFO

For information on careers and membership for high school and college students, contact
American Copy Editors Society
Seven Avenida Vista Grande, Suite B7
#467
Santa Fe, NM 87508-9207
415-704-4884
info@copydesk.org
http://www.copydesk.org

For information on editing and to read the *Magazine Handbook,* visit
American Society of Magazine Editors
810 Seventh Avenue, 24th Floor
New York, NY 10019-5873
212-872-3700
asme@magazine.org
http://www.magazine.org/asme

For career-related publications, visit the ASNE Web site.
American Society of News Editors (ASNE)
11690B Sunrise Valley Drive
Reston, VA 20191-1409
703-453-1122
asne@asne.org
http://www.asne.org

This membership organization seeks to improve the quality of journalism in sports newsrooms.
Associated Press Sports Editors
http://apsportseditors.org

This organization of book publishers offers an extensive Web site for people interested in learning more about the book business.
Association of American Publishers
71 Fifth Avenue, 2nd Floor
New York, NY 10003-3004
212-255-0200
http://www.publishers.org

For information on investigative journalism, contact
Investigative Reporters and Editors
Missouri School of Journalism
141 Neff Annex
Columbia, MO 65211-0001
573-882-2042
info@ire.org
http://www.ire.org

For information on careers in the newspaper industry, contact
Newspaper Association of America
4401 Wilson Boulevard, Suite 900
Arlington, VA 22203-1867
571-366-1000
http://www.naa.org

Environmental Writers

What Environmental Writers Do

Writers express their ideas in words for books, magazines, newspapers, advertisements, radio, television, films, and the Internet. Writers' jobs are a combination of creativity and hard work. *Environmental writers,* as you might have guessed, specialize in writing about the environment. They write about every environmental-related topic imaginable—from the daily habits of buffalo and bears, to recommended wildflower viewing areas in state and national parks, to ecofriendly vacation destinations, to serious issues that affect the environment such as deforestation, pollution, global warming, suburban sprawl, and threats to endangered species. Other environmental writers create scripts about nature and environmental issues for television, film, and radio documentaries.

Successful environmental writers are good researchers. Before they begin writing, they must gather as much information as possible about the topic of the article. They conduct research on the Internet and at libraries. They interview government officials, scientists, and environmental professionals. They also spend long hours of observation and personal experience at state and national parks, in laboratories, at sites that are polluted, and other places. After gathering their research, writers prepare an outline or summary that serves as a guide as they write the article. Then they begin writing. They write a first draft and then keep rewriting sections of the article until they believe they have conveyed the story or their opinions in the best possible manner. When they have finished the article,

EXPLORING

- Learn as much as you can about nature and the environment by contacting environmental associations and reading books and magazines about the environment.
- Read all kinds of writing—poetry, fiction, nonfiction, essays. Read books, newspapers, and magazines.
- Read books about writing. See the Browse and Learn More section at the end of this book for some suggestions.

- Take writing classes at school or at your local community center.
- Work as a reporter or writer on your school newspaper, literary magazine, or yearbook.
- Write essays and articles about environmental issues or a trip you took to a state or national park.
- Write every day. Keep a separate notebook just for journal writing.
- Talk to an environmental writer about his or her career.

they submit it to an *editor*, who reviews, corrects, and revises it many times before it is ready for publication.

Education and Training

In high school, take courses in English, literature, foreign languages, history, general science, environmental science, biology, chemistry, social studies, computer science, and typing.

A college education is usually necessary if you want to become an environmental writer. You should also know how to use a computer for word processing and be good at conducting research on the Internet. Some employers prefer to hire people who have a communications or journalism degree.

Others require majors in English, literature, history, philosophy, or one of the social sciences. Other environmental writers have degrees in environmental-related majors such as

Environmental activist and writer Robert Kennedy Jr., the son of the late Robert F. Kennedy, speaks at a rally calling for an end to mountaintop removal mining. (Bob Bird, AP Photo)

Helping Hands: Don Henley and The Walden Woods Project

Henry David Thoreau (1817–1862) was an American author and naturalist. His *Walden* (1854) is a classic of American literature. It tells about the two years he lived in a small cabin on the shore of Walden Pond near Concord, Massachusetts. In *Walden,* he described the changing seasons and other natural events and scenes that he observed in what became known as Walden Woods.

Because of Thoreau's writings, Walden Woods became a treasured place. Approximately 60 percent of the area was protected from development. But in the mid-1980s, developers decided to build condominiums and an office building on some of the unprotected areas. People were upset that these beautiful natural areas would be destroyed, but they did not have the money or power to stop the development. They feared that construction would begin.

Don Henley, an environmentalist and a member of the well-known rock group the Eagles, was also upset that the land was going to be developed. In 1990, he founded the Walden Woods Project to save the land from development. He used his fame and wealth to fund efforts to stop construction. He told everyone he could about what was happening to the land. People began to donate money to the fight and the news media began to cover the story. Within a few years, the land was purchased and saved from development.

Today, the majority of Walden Woods is protected from development. Nature-lovers from around the world visit Walden Woods to experience the natural world described in *Walden.*

Henley continues to use his wealth and fame to help protect our nation's natural wonders and educate people about environmental issues such as protecting wetlands and endangered species and improving the quality of our air and water.

Visit http://www.mass.gov/dcr/parks/walden to learn more about Walden Woods.

Source: The Walden Woods Project, http://www.walden.org

Tips for Success

To be a successful environmental writer, you should

- care deeply about the environment
- be creative
- have excellent writing skills
- be a good researcher
- have a curious personality
- have a good memory
- be able to work under deadline pressure

biology, environmental science, environmental engineering, or oceanography.

Some environmental writers learn their skills on their own. A few become successful without a college education, but most have attended at least some college-level courses. Classes and writing groups can be found almost anywhere, from community colleges to park districts to the Web.

Earnings

Salaries for all writers ranged from less than $29,000 to more than $109,000 in 2010, according to the U.S. Department of Labor. Writers employed by the newspaper, book, and directory publishing industries earned average salaries of about $56,000. Many creative writers work at other jobs and pursue creative writing on a part-time basis.

Outlook

Employment opportunities in writing are expected to be good over the next decade. Jobs should be available at newspapers, magazines, book publishers, advertising agencies, businesses, media companies, and nonprofit organizations. However, competition for jobs is very intense.

There are many environmental-related topics to write about. But it is important to keep in mind that only a small number of writers specialize in writing about the environment. Many write about a wide range of topics as part of their job duties. Writers with knowledge of many fields—not just the environment—will have the best job prospects.

FOR MORE INFO

For information on careers in science writing, contact

National Association of Science Writers
PO Box 7905
Berkeley, CA 94707-0905
510-647-9500
http://www.nasw.org

For information on editorial writing, contact

National Conference of Editorial Writers
3899 North Front Street
Harrisburg, PA 17110-1583
717-703-3015
ncew@pa-news.org
http://www.ncew.org

For information about working as a writer and union membership, contact

National Writers Union
256 West 38th Street, Suite 703
New York, NY 10018-9807
212-254-0279
http://www.nwu.org

For industry information, contact

North American Travel Journalists Association
3579 East Foothill Boulevard, No 744
Pasadena, CA 91107-3119

626-376-9754
http://www.natja.org

For information on contests for students in grades six through 12, contact

Outdoor Writers Association of America
615 Oak Street, Suite 201
Missoula, MT 59801-2469
406-728-7434
http://owaa.org

For information about travel writing, contact

Society of American Travel Writers
11950 West Lake Park Drive, Suite 320
Milwaukee, WI 52334-3049
414-359-1625
info@satw.org
http://www.satw.org

For information on journalism, contact

Society of Professional Journalists
Eugene S. Pulliam National Journalism Center
3909 North Meridian Street
Indianapolis, IN 46208-4011
317-927-8000
http://www.spj.org

Fashion Writers

What Fashion Writers Do

Fashion writers express their ideas about fashion in words for books, magazines, newspapers, radio, television, and the Internet. These writing jobs require a combination of creativity, hard work, and knowledge of fashion. Fashion writers are also known as *fashion reporters, journalists, correspondents,* and *authors.*

Most fashion writers work for fashion magazines. These writers report on fashion news, interview top designers, and write feature articles on the latest styles for a season (a time of the year when certain fashions are introduced to the public). Fashion writers also work for newspapers that have fashion sections (often a part of a larger arts-and-entertainment department), Web sites, or other media outlets. Other fashion writers work for book publishers.

To write a story, fashion writers obtain as much information as possible about the subject. They conduct research at libraries and on the Internet; interview fashion industry professionals in person, on the phone, and via e-mail; and attend fashion shows and other industry events. After gathering information, they create an outline that helps them to write a first draft. Then they write the article, rewriting sections until they find the best way to express their ideas. They review and rewrite the text until they decide it is ready to submit to an editor for publication.

Fashion editors work with fashion writers on the staffs of newspapers, magazines, publishing houses, radio or television stations, and corporations of all kinds. Their main job is to

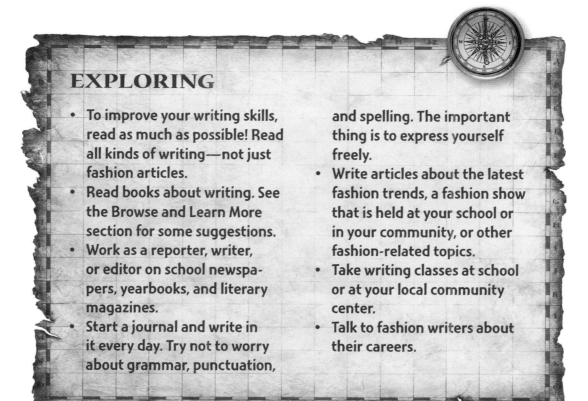

EXPLORING

- To improve your writing skills, read as much as possible! Read all kinds of writing—not just fashion articles.
- Read books about writing. See the Browse and Learn More section for some suggestions.
- Work as a reporter, writer, or editor on school newspapers, yearbooks, and literary magazines.
- Start a journal and write in it every day. Try not to worry about grammar, punctuation, and spelling. The important thing is to express yourself freely.
- Write articles about the latest fashion trends, a fashion show that is held at your school or in your community, or other fashion-related topics.
- Take writing classes at school or at your local community center.
- Talk to fashion writers about their careers.

make sure that text provided by fashion writers is suitable in content, format, and style for the intended audiences.

Education and Training

In high school, take English, journalism, and communications courses. To gain a better understanding of fashion and design, take classes in family and consumer science, including sewing and design, if they are available. The fashion industry is located throughout the world, so taking a foreign language such as French or Italian will also be helpful. Other useful courses include computer science and typing.

A college education is usually necessary if you want to become a writer. You should also know how to use a computer for word processing and be able to conduct research using the Internet. Employers prefer to hire people who have a communications, English, or journalism degree. Fashion writers must

Fashion Publications on the Web

- *CosmoGirl!*
  http://www.seventeen.com/cosmogirl
- *Cosmopolitan*
  http://www.cosmopolitan.com
- *ELLE*
  http://www.elle.com
- *ELLEgirl*
  http://ellegirl.elle.com
- *GQ*
  http://www.gq.com
- *Glamour*
  http://www.glamour.com
- *Harper's Bazaar*
  http://www.harpersbazaar.com
- *InStyle*
  http://www.instyle.com
- *The New York Times: Fashion & Style*
  http://www.nytimes.com/pages/fashion
- *Vogue*
  http://www.vogue.com
- *W*
  http://www.wmagazine.com
- *Women's Wear Daily*
  http://www.wwd.com

know a lot about their subject, so classes in fashion design and marketing are also useful. Some writers may have a college degree in fashion or a related field in addition to a degree in English, journalism, or communications.

Earnings

Beginning fashion writers earn salaries that range from $20,000 to $25,000 per year. Most reporters, a category that includes fashion writers, earned between $20,000 and $75,000 a year in 2010, according to the U.S. Department of Labor. Well-known writers can earn more than $100,000 per year, but they are few in number.

Tips for Success

To be a successful fashion writer, you should

- have excellent writing skills
- be a good researcher
- be an expert at grammar and punctuation
- have strong communication skills
- have a working knowledge of clothing construction and the fashion industry
- be willing to stay current with the latest trends in the industry
- be able to meet deadlines

Outlook

Employment for writers is expected to be good during the next decade. Jobs should be available at newspapers, magazines, book publishers, advertising agencies, businesses, Web sites, and nonprofit organizations. Despite this prediction, it will be hard to land a job as a fashion writer since many people want to enter the field. Those with previous experience and specialized education in fashion and reporting will have the best chances of finding jobs.

FOR MORE INFO

This organization of book publishers offers an extensive Web site for people interested in learning more about the book business.

Association of American Publishers
71 Fifth Avenue, 2nd Floor
New York, NY 10003-3004
212-255-0200
http://www.publishers.org

For industry information, contact
Fashion Group International Inc.
8 West 40th Street, 7th Floor
New York, NY 10018-2276
212-302-5511
http://www.fgi.org

This organization is a good source of information about the magazine industry.

Magazine Publishers of America
810 Seventh Avenue, 24th Floor
New York, NY 10019-5873
212-872-3700
mpa@magazine.org
http://www.magazine.org

For information on educational programs in fashion, contact
National Association of Schools of Art and Design
11250 Roger Bacon Drive, Suite 21
Reston, VA 20190-5248
703-437-0700
info@arts-accredit.org
http://nasad.arts-accredit.org

Food Writers

What Food Writers Do

Food writers deal with the written word, whether the completed work is the printed page, broadcast, or computer screen. They write about all things related to food and beverages. This includes recipes, new food products, meal planning and preparation, grocery shopping, cooking utensils and related products, places that serve food and beverages, and famous chefs. The nature of their work is as varied as the materials they produce: magazines, newspapers, books, trade journals and other publications, text for Web sites, advertisements, and scripts for radio and television broadcast. The one common factor is the subject: food.

Food writers need to be able to write very descriptively, since the reader will not be able to taste, touch, or smell the product they are writing about. Depending on whether or not pictures or videos accompany the written word, the reader may not even be able to see it. Food writers use their writing skills to write about many different things. They might write a press release about a new food product to be distributed to food editors at numerous newspapers and magazines. They may write a story about seasonal fruits and vegetables for a local television news broadcast. They may write an article for a women's magazine about new cooking utensils that make meal preparation easier for amateur chefs. They may write a review about a new restaurant that just opened.

EXPLORING

- Take writing classes at school or at your local community center.
- Explore your love for food and increase your knowledge by taking cooking classes, attending ethnic festivals and food events, or touring different food-related businesses.
- Read books about the art of writing. See the Browse and Learn More section for some suggestions.
- Visit recipe Web sites. Here are a few suggestions: KidsHealth: Recipes (http://kidshealth.org/kid/recipes), Recipe Source (http://www.recipesource.com), Food Network (http://www.foodnetwork.com), and MarthaStewart.com (http://www.marthastewart.com/food).

- Experiment with different types of restaurants and cuisines. After dining at a new restaurant, write about the experience. Review your writing. It is objective? Descriptive? Informative? Edit and rewrite it until you are satisfied with your work.
- Work as a reporter for your high school or community newspaper.
- Professional organizations dedicated to food writing, such as those listed at the end of this article, often provide information, resources, conferences, and other guidance programs that may be of interest to you.
- Ask a teacher or counselor to arrange an information interview with a food writer.

Some popular specialties include cookbook writers, recipe writers, and critics. The following paragraphs provide an overview of these careers.

Cookbook writers write cookbooks. They may work as staff writers for a book publisher or be self-employed. To write a cookbook, cookbook writers need to first decide what type of cookbook they would like to write. Do they want to write a general cookbook that covers every course in a meal (such as appetizers, salads, breads, soups, meats, vegetables, and desserts) or a cookbook that focuses on one ingredient (lobster, for example) or one course (such as soup)? Do they want to write a regional cookbook (about food from a particular region in the United States or world)? An ethnic cookbook (focusing on food from Italy, Japan, Mexico, or another culture)? Or an appliance- or equipment-related cookbook (focusing on cooking with a bread machine, microwave oven, or outdoor grill)?

Once they have decided what type of cookbook to write, cookbook writers develop the various sections of the cookbook. They create a rough outline, which details the features (recipes, of course, but perhaps a glossary and other resources) that will be included in the book. Then they develop their recipe ideas. Recipes are a set of instructions that people use to prepare a food dish. They prepare each recipe many times to ensure that they have accurately presented measurements, portion sizes, ingredients, and any other component that may make or break a recipe. As they prepare the recipe, they take notes on the process for later review. The recipe development process will be much easier if the cookbook writer is comfortable in the kitchen and familiar with cooking techniques.

As they create and test the recipes, cookbook writers may also begin working on the other sections in the book. This allows them to tie in all of the various segments of the book so that they make sense to the readers. The table of contents details the various sections in the book. The writer creates it by referring to the original outline. The introduction covers the focus of the book and, perhaps, the writer's personal reasons for writing the book. A how-to section gives the reader instructions on how to do a specific task, such as how to cut meat or

Food writer Nigella Lawson signs a book for a fan. (Amy Sussman, AP Photo/ Graylock.com)

dice vegetables. The glossary contains definitions of cooking-related terms, such as broil, blend, and baste. The bibliography lists other books and articles that the writer referred to as he or she wrote the book.

Recipe writers create recipes for books, magazines, newspapers, Web sites, and any other publication or product that features food-related articles and recipes. Recipes typically have the following components: the name of the dish, the amount of time needed to prepare the dish, the ingredients (usually listed in the order that they will be used), the equipment (stove, microwave, blender, baking pans, etc.), an ordered list of preparation instructions, and the number of servings the recipe will make. Recipe writers may also include information about the region or culture from which the recipe originated, nutritional information (including calories, fat content, etc.), and potential variations (such as a low-fat or low-carb version of the recipe) or substitutions (such as using skim milk instead of whole milk) that the reader may use when preparing the dish.

To create a useful recipe, recipe writers should explain every step, ingredient, and preparation process in detail. This helps readers to prepare the recipe as easily as possible. They should also prepare their finished recipe many times to ensure that it contains no errors or confusing instructions.

Perhaps the most infamous type of food writer is the *food/restaurant critic*. The critic needs to be fair with any type of product or restaurant review. When dining at a restaurant, he or she also needs to be anonymous (hide their identity), which is not always easy. While dining, food/restaurant critics need to make accurate observations and try to write or record them without arousing the suspicion of the restaurant staff, lest they realize they were being reviewed and adjust the level of service or quality.

The work of food writers is reviewed and edited by *food editors.* They correct grammar, spelling, and style. They check all the facts, especially where recipes are concerned. Editors make sure that the writing follows style guidelines, and that the writing is appropriate for the intended audience.

Education and Training

If you are interested in becoming a food writer, take English, general science, family and consumer science, and computer classes while in high school. If they are offered, take classes in writing, such as journalism, creative writing, and business communications. Writers must be expert communicators, so you should excel in English. While in high school, working on your school's newspaper, yearbook, or any other publication will be of benefit to you.

Food Magazines on the Web

- *Bon Appetit*
  http://www.bonappetit.com
- *Cook's Illustrated*
  http://www.cooksillustrated.com
- *Fine Cooking*
  http://www.finecooking.com
- *Gourmet*
  http://www.gourmet.com

FOR MORE INFO

Visit this organization's Web site for information on issues facing food writers.

Association of Food Journalists
7 Avenida Vista Grande, Suite B7, #467
Santa Fe, NM 87508-9207
http://www.afjonline.com

To read *The Journalist's Road to Success: A Career Guide*, visit the DJNF Web site.

Dow Jones News Fund (DJNF)
PO Box 300
Princeton, NJ 08543-0300
609-452-2820
djnf@dowjones.com
https://www.newsfund.org

This organization provides a wealth of industry information at its Web site.

International Association of Culinary Professionals
1100 Johnson Ferry Road, Suite 300
Atlanta, GA 30342-1733

404-252-3663
info@iacp.com
http://www.iacp.com

This organization offers an online newsletter and magazine at its Web site.

International Food, Wine & Travel Writers Association
1142 South Diamond Bar Boulevard, #177
Diamond Bar, CA 91765-2203
877-439-8929
admin@ifwtwa.org
http://www.ifwtwa.org

For information on the magazine industry, contact

Magazine Publishers of America
810 Seventh Avenue, 24th Floor
New York, NY 10019-5873
212-872-3700
mpa@magazine.org
http://www.magazine.org

Most food writing jobs require a college education. Some employers want new hires to have communications or journalism degrees. Most schools offer courses in journalism and some have more specialized courses in book publishing, publication management, and newspaper and magazine writing. Some offer majors or minors in food writing.

Some employers require a degree or certificate from culinary school, or culinary work experience, in addition to a background in writing. You may wish to take cooking classes at a local culinary school or community college to improve your chances of landing a job as a food writer.

Earnings

The International Association of Culinary Professionals compiled a list of salaries for careers in the culinary field, including the following: cookbook author, $5,000 to $10,000 for their first book; food writer on staff at a publication, $19,000 to $40,000 annually; and freelance food writer, $100 to $1,000 per story. In general, salaries are higher in large cities.

In addition to their salaries, many food writers receive other types of compensation. Most food critics, for example, have the meals they eat at a restaurant for the purpose of a review paid for by their employer. Some food writers also receive travel expenses to cover costs such as mileage from driving to cover local events, or airfare and hotel rooms for covering out-of-town industry events.

Outlook

Employment for all writers is expected to be good during the next decade. Employment will not be as strong for food writers. Individuals entering this field should realize that the competition for jobs is intense. Students just out of college may especially have trouble finding employment. However, the subject of food and beverages continues to grow in popularity, thus providing more opportunities for those who wish to pursue a career in food writing.

Grant Writers

What Grant Writers Do

It takes a lot of money to run a school, social service agency, or other nonprofit organization. In many instances, these organizations try to find outside sources for money to run their operations. To obtain funding, these organizations must apply for financial grants from government agencies or private foundations. To do so, they employ *grant writers* to write grant proposals.

The grant proposal is a document in which a nonprofit organization lists its reasons for wanting outside funding. The grant writer makes it clear to the funding agency why the project is important and how the money will be spent. For example, a grant writer writing a proposal for a high school that wants a new computer lab must explain why obtaining the money to build the lab is important. They would cite the importance of young people learning about computers and preparing for college and careers. They might also note that the computers in the existing lab are too old to meet the needs of students or that that it is too small to serve a large number of students. Also in the proposal, the grant writer must describe both the short-term and long-term goals of the organization so that an outsider can understand them. The grant writer must write different

EXPLORING

- Develop your skills in research and writing.
- Volunteer for nonprofit organizations to find out about a grant writer's work firsthand.
- Talk to a grant writer about his or her career.

DID YOU KNOW?

The first recorded government research grant was given to the inventor Samuel Morse in 1842. In the United States, the amount of grants funding has grown consistently and dramatically since that time. More private foundations began giving grants when it became clear how much help they could provide to all types of nonprofit groups. Government agencies have increased grants funding, especially in the sciences. These grants help U.S. scientists and inventors stay on the cutting edge of new technology.

DID YOU KNOW?

Where Grant Writers Work

- Arts organizations
- Cultural centers
- Educational institutions
- Museums
- Research foundations
- Self-employment
- Social service agencies

proposals for different kinds of funding. For example, an organization might need money for general operations or it might need funds for a specific program or project.

If a grant application is accepted, the grant writer must often write follow-up reports to inform the funding agency how the money was spent.

Education and Training

If you want to become a grant writer, you should take courses in English, journalism, and creative writing to develop your written communication skills. Courses in history and social studies also are useful.

More and more colleges and universities are offering classes that teach the grant application process. There are also a number of organizations that give workshops on grant proposal writing. These workshops teach you how to research funding organizations and how to prepare proposals.

Earnings

Grant writers earned median annual salaries of $56,698 in July 2010, according to Salary.com. Those just starting out in the field earned less than $43,000, while the most experienced workers earned more than $72,000. Some grant writers are paid by the hour. The American Grant Writers' Association reports that grant writ-

FOR MORE INFO

Contact the following organizations for information on grantwriting and fund-raising:

American Grant Writers' Association
PO Box 8481
Seminole, FL 33775-8481
727-366-9334
customerservice@agwa.us
http://www.agwa.us

Association of Fundraising Professionals
4300 Wilson Boulevard, Suite 300
Arlington, VA 22203-4179
800-666-3863
http://www.afpnet.org

CFRE International
300 North Washington Street, Suite 504
Alexandria, VA 22314-2535

703-820-5555
info@cfre.org
http://www.cfre.org

Giving Institute: Leading Consultants to Non-Profits
303 West Madison Street, Suite 2650
Chicago, IL 60606-3396
312-981-6794
info@givinginstitute.org
http://www.aafrc.org

The Grantsmanship Center
PO Box 17220
Los Angeles, CA 90017-0220
213-482-9860
info@tgci.com
http://www.tgci.com

ers receive anywhere from $40 to $100 per hour for researching grant opportunities and writing proposals.

Outlook

There should continue to be steady employment opportunities for grant writers. A skilled grant writer can be the difference between an organization obtaining funding or not. Opportunities will be best for grant writers with a proven track record of writing successful grant proposals.

What Literary Agents Do

Literary agents work for writers. They try to sell writers' works to publishers and film and television producers. Clients of literary agents might include new or established authors, or actors, athletes, musicians, and other public figures who want to be authors. To give their clients more time to write and revise their work, agents sometimes manage writers' business affairs. This might involve bookkeeping tasks and preparing tax forms. Literary agents are also called *authors' agents* and *writers' representatives*.

Literary agents begin by reading and evaluating writers' manuscripts. Then they decide whether to represent those writers. Agents might suggest revisions to improve the manuscripts and make them more marketable. They contact editors, publishers, and producers and try to sell their clients' work to them. Editors and producers may also make certain suggestions about manuscripts, and the agent gives this information to the client.

After selling a client's manuscript, the literary agent negotiates a contract, working out pay rates and

EXPLORING

- Learn about current trends in book publishing and the kinds of books that particular publishing houses issue.
- Read magazines such as *Publishers Weekly* (http://www.publishersweekly.com) to learn more about the industry.
- Part-time or volunteer work at bookstores and libraries will help you become familiar with books and publishers.
- Talk to a literary agent about his or her career.

deadlines when chapters or entire articles are due. They also may create publicity and schedule public appearances (such as a reading at a book store or book fair), depending on the nature of the written work and the author's popularity.

Literary agents must spend a great deal of time and effort on their work. They carefully read manuscripts. They establish and maintain good business relationships with publishers and producers. They study the literary and dramatic markets. Most literary agents often have to work evenings and weekends to meet with clients and potential buyers.

Literary agents work for agencies of all sizes. Most agents are based in Los Angeles or New York because of the many publishing companies and film and television studios in those cities. Literary agencies also have branch offices in other cities. Experienced literary agents may travel around the country or

Words to Learn

advance the amount of money paid to an author before the book is published; authors usually receive one-half of this amount when they sign the contract and the other half when they turn in the final manuscript

boilerplate a standard contract; most authors and agents make many changes to the boilerplate before it is signed

contract a legal agreement between two parties

copyright a legal means to protect an author's work; it recog-nizes the author as owner of the writing and gives the author the right to decide how the work will be used

manuscript a document created by a writer, typically a book, article, or script

negotiation a series of written and/or verbal exchanges between two parties to determine the legal terms of a contract

royalties a percentage of the profits from the sale of a book paid to the author

DID YOU KNOW?

Agents charge different fees, but usually they receive a 15 percent commission on the books they sell and everything relating to that book. This includes magazine articles, audio recordings, and films. Agents usually receive 20 percent for overseas sales. Part of this percentage goes to the overseas agent.

A few agents charge a reading fee just for looking at a writer's work. Many agents also charge for long distance phone calls, photocopying, messenger services, and other small expenses.

Agents don't always charge a commission. Some review and market a book proposal on an hourly fee basis. They earn a fee whether they sell the proposal or not.

Source: Adler & Robin Books Inc.

even around the world to meet with clients and with buyers. Some literary agents are self-employed. They own their own businesses.

Education and Training

High school students who are interested in this type of career should take courses in business, marketing, literature, composition, speech, and drama.

There are no formal or specific requirements for becoming a literary agent. A college degree, however, is a plus. In college, it is helpful to take classes in the liberal arts and business administration. Communications courses also will help you interact with clients and buyers. Some literary agents earn law degrees.

Many literary agents start out as journalists or editors. As they work with more and more authors during their careers, they become interested in representing them and selling authors' works to publishers. If they become literary agents through this route, they would earn degrees in journalism, English, or communications in college.

Earnings

Those who begin their careers in an entry-level position with an agency might earn as much as an average office worker. At higher levels, earnings almost always are based on commission, which means that the agent will be paid a rate based on what the client earns. The standard rate is 4 percent to 20 percent of the client's earnings. Salaries range from $20,000 to $60,000. A few agents make hundreds of thousands of dollars. Experienced literary agents with successful clients and good reputations earn the most money.

FOR MORE INFO

For information on the duties, responsibilities, and ethical expectations of agents, and for AAR's newsletter, contact or visit the following Web site:
Association of Authors' Representatives, Inc. (AAR)
676-A Ninth Avenue, Suite 312
New York, NY 10036-3602
administrator@aaronline.org
http://aaronline.org

Outlook

Competition is very strong among literary agents. Many people who want to become agents do not succeed. Those who do succeed may be employed by a literary agency, working their way from an entry-level position to one of great responsibility. The very talented and hardworking eventually may become self-employed. They open their own literary agencies.

Movie Writers and Critics

What Movie Writers and Critics Do

"That movie was great!" "No, it stunk!" "It was OK, but I really liked..." Everyone seems to have an opinion about movies today. But did you know that some people make a career out of writing and talking about movies? *Movie writers* express their ideas about movies in words for books, magazines, newspapers, advertisements, radio, television, and the Internet. These writing jobs require a combination of creativity and hard work. Movie writers are also known as *movie reporters* and *authors*. (For information about writers who create scripts for films, see the article on Screenwriters.)

To write an interesting and informative article, movie writers have to gather a lot of information. They conduct interviews with actors, directors, and other movie industry workers. They visit movie sets. They watch a lot of movies. They also conduct research at libraries and on the Internet. Once they have completed their research, they prepare an outline or summary of what they want to say in the article. This outline helps them to write a first draft. Then they begin writing. They keep revising the article in order to best express their ideas. Generally, their writing will be reviewed, corrected, and revised many times by an *editor* before a final copy is ready for publication.

Movie critics review films for print publications, Web sites, and television and radio stations. They review all types of new movies—from comedies and dramas, to documentaries and foreign films, to animated shorts. Critics watch the movies they plan to review at special screenings or via advance DVD copies

EXPLORING

- Take writing classes at school or at your local community center.
- To improve your writing skills, read, read, read! Read all kinds of writing—not just movie articles and reviews. Fiction, nonfiction, poetry, and essays will introduce you to many different forms of writing.
- Read books about writing. See the Browse and Learn More section for some suggestions.
- Work as a reporter, writer, or editor on school newspapers, yearbooks, and literary magazines.
- Start a journal and write in it every day. Write about or review movies and television shows that you have watched.
- Talk to movie writers and critics about their careers.

that they can view at home or in the office. When reviewing a movie, a critic takes into account many factors. Critics analyze the storyline; performance of the actors; quality of the movie's direction, editing, and special effects; and overall entertainment value. They determine if the movie met standards they have established in these categories. Then they usually assign a rating to the movie. Their reviews are read or listened to by many people who want advice on what movie to see.

Education and Training

In high school, take English, journalism, and communications courses. To gain a better understanding of movies, take classes in broadcasting and film, if they are available. Other useful courses include computer science and typing.

Movie critic Roger Ebert poses for photographers during a ceremony that honored him with a star on the Hollywood Walk of Fame. (Ric Francis, AP Photo)

DID YOU KNOW?

Opening Soon at a Theater Near You was the first film review television show in the United States. It debuted on September 4, 1975, and was hosted by movie critics Roger Ebert and Gene Siskel. *Opening Soon* started as a local show on WTTW, a public broadcasting station in Chicago. In 1977, the show went national, and its name was changed to *Sneak Previews*. The show was very popular during its time, and aired on more than 180 stations. *Sneak Previews* made stars out of Roger Ebert and Gene Siskel. They became some of the most well-known movie critics in the world. Gene Siskel passed away in 1999. Roger Ebert continues to review movies for the *Chicago Sun-Times,* and writes books about the movie industry. Visit http://rogerebert.suntimes.com to read Ebert's movie reviews.

A college education is usually necessary if you want to become a writer or critic. You should also know how to use a computer for word processing and be able to handle the pressure of deadlines. Employers prefer to hire people who have a communications, English, or journalism degree. Movie writers and critics must know a lot about their subject, so film classes are also useful. Some writers and editors may have a college degree in film, drama, film directing, film production, or a related field in addition to a degree in English, journalism, or communications.

Tips for Success

To be a successful movie writer or critic, you should

- have a strong love of and interest in movies
- have excellent writing skills
- be opinionated
- be a good researcher
- be an expert at grammar and punctuation
- have strong communication skills
- be able to meet deadlines
- enjoy meeting and interacting with others
- be willing to accept criticism from the public, who may not agree with your opinions

FOR MORE INFO

Visit the association's Web site to learn more about the book business.
Association of American Publishers
71 Fifth Avenue, 2nd Floor
New York, NY 10003-3004
212-255-0200
http://www.publishers.org

This organization is a good source of information about the magazine industry.
Association of Magazine Media
810 Seventh Avenue, 24th Floor
New York, NY 10019-5873
212-872-3700
mpa@magazine.org
http://www.magazine.org

The association represents nearly 200 television, radio, and online critics in the United States and Canada.
Broadcast Film Critics Association
9220 Sunset Boulevard, Suite 220
Los Angeles, CA 90069-3503
310-860-2665
info@bfca.org
http://criticschoice.com

For information on the Golden Globe Awards, contact
Hollywood Foreign Press Association
646 North Robertson Boulevard
West Hollywood, CA 90069-5022
info@hfpa.org
http://www.goldenglobes.org

For information on careers in the newspaper industry, contact
Newspaper Association of America
4401 Wilson Boulevard, Suite 900
Arlington, VA 22203-1867
571-366-1000
http://www.naa.org

The OFCS is an international association of Internet-based film critics and journalists.
Online Film Critics Society (OFCS)
gc@ofcs.org
http://www.ofcs.org

Visit the following Web site for detailed information about journalism careers:
High School Journalism
http://www.hsj.org

Earnings

Most writers earned between $29,000 and $78,000 a year in 2010, according to the U.S. Department of Labor (DOL). Top writers can earn more than $110,000 a year. Some movie writers work part time and are paid per article or review.

The DOL loosely categorizes critics under the heading of reporter. According to the DOL, the median annual salary for reporters was $34,360 in 2009. Salaries ranged from less than $20,000 to $745,000 or more. In the same year, reporters who worked in radio and television broadcasting had average annual earnings of $53,590. Those employed by newspaper, periodical, book, and directory publishers earned $38,420.

Outlook

Many people want to become movie writers and critics. This makes it difficult to land a job in the field—especially because there are only a small number of positions available. Writers and critics with previous experience and specialized education in film studies and reporting will have the best chances of finding jobs.

Press Secretaries and Political Consultants

What Press Secretaries Do

Press secretaries, political consultants, and other media relations professionals help politicians promote themselves and their issues to voters. Television ads, radio spots, Twitter accounts, social networking Web sites, and campaign Web sites are important for candidates running for office. Once elected to office, politicians need press secretaries to answer the questions of journalists, write speeches, and organize press conferences.

Press secretaries serve on the congressional staffs of senators and representatives, or in the office of the president or other government officials. They write press releases and opinion pieces to tell the public about the efforts of the government officials they work for. They also schedule press conferences, and prepare their employer for interviews. Press secretaries also work for corporations and for organizations and nonprofit groups that have legislative concerns.

Political consultants help produce radio, TV, and Internet ads. They write campaign plans and develop themes for these campaigns. A theme may focus on a spe-

White House press secretary Jay Carney briefs reporters at the White House.
(Charles Dharapak, AP Photo)

cific issue (such as gun control or the environment), or on the differences between a politician and his or her opponent. Consultants may be hired for an entire campaign, or they may be hired only to produce one ad or to come up with a catchy quote for the media.

Political consultants are often called *spin doctors* because of their ability to manipulate the media, or put a good spin on a news story that best suits the purposes of their clients. Using newspapers, radio and TV broadcasts, and the Internet, political consultants, press secretaries, and other media representatives try to focus on a politician's good qualities and downplay any negative publicity. During very sensitive times, such as during scandals, wars, or after unpopular political decisions, media representatives must answer questions carefully. Many media representatives are responsible for bringing public attention to important issues. They help develop support for school funding, environmental concerns, and other community needs.

Education and Training

In high school, you should take journalism, English, history, and political science classes. English composition, drama, and speech classes will help you develop good communication skills. Government, history, and civics classes will teach you about the structure of government.

Most people in media relations have bachelor's degrees, and some also hold master's degrees, doctorates, and law degrees. Some of the majors you should consider as an undergraduate are journalism, political science, public relations, English, marketing, and economics.

Tips for Success

To be a successful press secretary or political consultant, you should

- have excellent communication skills
- be able to keep your cool under pressure
- be very organized
- be able to handle many tasks at the same time
- be an expert in politics
- have good problem-solving skills
- have a confident personality

Earnings

Public relations specialists (a career category that includes press secretaries) had median annual earnings of $52,090 in 2010, according to the U.S. Department of Labor. Salaries ranged from less than $31,000 to more than $95,000. In 2010, mean earnings for those who worked in local government were $56,050. The earnings of political consultants vary greatly. Someone who works with local candidates or with

Profile: James C. Hagerty (1909–1981)

President Dwight D. Eisenhower's press secretary was James C. Hagerty. People still talk about him as a legend, and the media consider him the standard by which all press secretaries are judged, according to Michael J. Towle, author of *On Behalf of the President: Four Factors Affecting the Success of the Presidential Press Secretary*. Eisenhower trusted Hagerty so much that when the president had a heart attack in 1955, he supposedly said, "Tell Jim to take over."

Hagerty was so honest and forthright with reporters about the president's condition that there was no room for guessing how the president was doing.

Journalists had a great deal of respect for Hagerty. James Deakin, White House reporter for the *St Louis Post-Dispatch*, wrote, "He was the best presidential press secretary who ever lived." The *New York Times* wrote, "Mr. Hagerty has raised the status of his post to that of a major administration official."

state-level political organizations and associations can make around $40,000 to $50,000 a year. Someone who works for high-profile candidates at the national level (such as those seeking to become U.S. senators or the president) can make more than $200,000.

Outlook

In recent years, press secretaries and consultants have become more and more important to candidates and elected officials. Television ads and Internet campaigns have become necessary in reaching the public. The jobs of press secretaries will expand as more news networks and news magazines report on the decisions and actions of government officials. Since news is reported 24 hours a day, seven days a week, press secretaries and political consultants will increasingly be needed to create positive press coverage for their employers.

FOR MORE INFO

For information about work as a political consultant, contact

American Association of Political Consultants
8400 Westpark Drive, 2nd Floor
McLean, VA 22102-5116
703-245-8020
info@theaapc.org
http://www.theaapc.org

Visit the Web sites of the House and the Senate for press releases and links to sites for individual members of Congress. To write to your state representatives, contact

Office of Congressperson (Name)
U.S. House of Representatives
Washington, DC 20515-0001
202-224-3121
http://www.house.gov

Office of Senator (Name)
United States Senate
Washington, DC 20510-0001
202-224-3121
http://www.senate.gov

Public Relations Specialists

What Public Relations Specialists Do

When a company or an organization wants to present a good image to the public, it often turns to its public relations department or to a public relations firm. *Public relations specialists* include executives, writers, artists, and researchers. These specialists work together to provide information to the public about an organization's goals and accomplishments and about its future plans or projects. Public relations specialists are sometimes called *publicists.*

Companies and organizations also rely on public relations specialists in times of crisis. For example, in the event of an environmental disaster, such as an oil spill, an oil company hires public relations specialists to help explain to the public what the company is doing to fix the problem. They also explain the steps the company is taking to help the people and natural areas that have been affected by the oil spill.

Public relations specialists spend much of their time writing. They write press releases, reports, news releases, booklets, speeches, copy for radio and television, and film scripts. Public relations specialists also edit employee publications, newsletters, and reports to shareholders. All of this writing and editing has one goal: to offer the public positive information about a person or company.

Contact with the media is another important part of the public relations specialists' jobs. They use news conference, radio, television, newspapers, magazines, and the Internet to pass along information. They also use special events to get their

EXPLORING

- Visit the Web site (http://www.prmuseum.com) of the Museum of Public Relations to read about early public relations pioneers.
- Almost any experience in working successfully with other people will help you to develop strong interpersonal skills, which are important in public relations.

- Take writing classes at school or at your local community center.
- Work as a volunteer on a political campaign to learn persuasive techniques.
- Any teaching or speaking experience will help you learn how to organize a presentation and talk to a group of people.
- Talk to a public relations specialist about his or her career.

messages across. Press parties, open houses, exhibits at conventions, and speeches help to establish good feelings and a positive image.

Some companies have their own public relations departments and hire their own workers. Other companies hire public relations firms whose workers provide public relations services to one or more companies. In either case, public relations specialists work closely with top executives to decide how to keep or improve a company's good image. Public relations workers sometimes do research or conduct public opinion polls. Then they develop a plan and put it into action.

Some public relations workers specialize in one area of public relations. One type of specialized public relations worker is the *lobbyist.* Lobbyists try to persuade elected officials to pass laws that will benefit their clients.

A publicist answers questions from the media during a press conference.
(Damian Dovarganes, AP Photo)

Education and Training

Most public relations specialists are college graduates. In high school you should take college-preparatory courses, especially English, speech, business, and foreign languages. Writing is an important part of public relations, so you should build your writing skills, perhaps by working on school publications.

In college, you should pursue a degree in public relations, English, or journalism. A graduate degree is often required for top managerial positions. Many students participate in an internship at a public relations firm to gain experience in the field and make valuable contacts.

Some companies have training programs for newly hired public relations specialists. In other companies, new employees work closely under the supervision of a more experienced specialist. They read and file newspaper and magazine articles, research, and learn to write press releases.

Fame & Fortune: Edward Bernays (1891–1995)

Edward Bernays was a groundbreaking U.S. publicist. He is often referred to as the "father of public relations." As soon as he entered the field, he wanted to be more than a publicist. He wanted to shape the public's interests to benefit the interests of his clients.

Bernays's first public relations job in 1913 was to help gather positive support for a controversial health movie. He often used strong methods of persuasion to influence public opinion. For example, working with a hairnet company, Bernays convinced prominent women that longer hair was more attractive. At the same time, he helped authorities recognize the dangers of factory workers wearing their long hair loose while on the job. These shaped opinions helped sell hairnets.

Bernays also used statistics from third parties in many of his campaigns.

In the 1920's he surveyed hospitals and found their preference for the unscented white soap over those with color and perfume. This preference was heavily marketed in favor of his client, Procter and Gamble, who happened to sell Ivory, an unscented, white soap.

Bernays worked for a variety of clients and companies, including the electric industry, General Motors, Columbia University, as well as the U.S. Armed Forces during World War II.

After retiring, Bernays continued to lecture on the topic of public relations at colleges and universities throughout the United States. *Life* magazine named him one of the 100 most influential Americans of the 20th century.

Source: Museum of Public Relations, Answers.com

Earnings

Public relations specialists earned median salaries of $52,090 in 2010, according to the U.S. Department of Labor. Those just starting out in the field earned less than $31,000 a year. Very experienced public relations specialists at large companies can make more than $250,000 a year.

Outlook

There will be excellent employment opportunities for public relations specialists during the next decade. Many companies are realizing that a good relationship with the public is key to selling their products or services. If people have a positive opinion of a company, they are more apt to be a customer. The public is just as likely to avoid a company or organization that does not have a good public image.

Most large companies have some sort of public relations resource, either through their own staff or through the use of outside consultants. More of the smaller companies are also hiring public relations specialists.

Workers who speak at least one foreign language and who are skilled at using social media will have the best job prospects.

DID YOU KNOW?

The first public relations counsel was a reporter named Ivy Ledbetter Lee. In 1906, he was named press representative for coal-mine operators. Labor disputes were becoming a large concern of the operators. They had problems because they refused to talk to the press and the hired miners. Lee convinced the mine operators to start answering press questions and give the press information on the mine's activities.

FOR MORE INFO

For industry information, contact
Automotive Public Relations Council
1301 West Long Lake, Suite 225
Troy, MI 48098-6371
248-952-6401, ext. 225
http://www.autopr.org

For career information and public relations news, contact
Council of Public Relations Firms
317 Madison Avenue, Suite 2320
New York, NY 10017-5205
877-773-4767
http://www.prfirms.org

Contact the association for information on accreditation for public relations specialists and related workers.
International Association of Business Communicators
601 Montgomery Street, Suite 1900
San Francisco, CA 94111-2623
415-544-4700
http://www.iabc.com

For information on school public relations, contact

National School Public Relations Association
15948 Derwood Road
Rockville, MD 20855-2123
301-519-0496
info@nspra.org
http://www.nspra.org

Visit the society's Web site for salary surveys, publications, and a blog about public relations.
Public Relations Society of America
33 Maiden Lane, 11th Floor
New York, NY 10038-5150
212-460-1400
http://www.prsa.org

For information on opportunities in Canada, contact
Canadian Public Relations Society
4195 Dundas Street West, Suite 346
Toronto, ON M8X 1Y4 Canada
416-239-7034
admin@cprs.ca
http://www.cprs.ca

Reporters and Correspondents

What Reporters and Correspondents Do

Reporters gather information and report the news for radio, television, magazines, newspapers, and Web sites. They cover local, national, or international news events.

Reporters gather all the information they need to write or broadcast clear and accurate news stories. They interview people, research the facts and history behind a story, observe important events, and then write the story. News stories may be a one-day item, such as a power failure or weather-related piece. Or they may cover a period of days or weeks, on subjects such as trials, investigations, major disasters, and government issues.

To gather information, reporters take notes and record interviews with news sources. Reporters may also examine documents related to the story. Before reporters start putting together their stories, they discuss the importance of the subject matter with an *editor* or a *producer.* Editors and producers decide what news will be covered each day. They determine how long a story should be and how much importance to give it. Sometimes they decide to hold the story for a while or not to run it at all.

Reporters then organize the information and write a concise, informative story. Reporters who are too far from their editorial office to return to file their reports may phone, email, or fax it in. Television reporters may broadcast from the scene of a story by using satellite or Internet technology.

EXPLORING

- Read your local newspaper regularly. Follow the work of one or two reporters who cover a topic that interests you, such as politics, science, or culture.
- Visit Web sites that offer international news. See the Browse and Learn More section for some suggestions.
- Talk to reporters and editors at local newspapers and radio and TV stations or interview journalism teachers at the school of journalism closest to your home. Ask a teacher or counselor to help you arrange the interviews.
- Work on your school newspaper or on a church, synagogue, or mosque newsletter.
- If you are lucky to take a trip abroad with your parents, keep a journal to record your experiences. Perhaps your school newspaper will publish your reports.

Because of continual deadline pressure, a reporter's life is hectic. Stories for nightly news broadcasts have to be in and reviewed by the producer before airtime. Newspaper articles must be filed long before the first edition is printed, which is usually in the very early hours of the morning. If a major news story takes place, reporters may have to work 18 or 20 hours without a break.

Correspondents are reporters who cover stories from a specific geographic or topical area. The two main types of correspondents are domestic and foreign correspondents.

Domestic correspondents usually cover one specific area of the news, such as politics, health, sports, consumer affairs, business, or religion. They are experts in that particular area and are counted on to provide detailed reporting about their specialty.

Foreign correspondents report on news from other countries or regions. Foreign news can range from wars, political takeovers (called coups), and refugee situations to cultural events and financial issues. Foreign correspondents usually cover all of these topics in the country or region where they are stationed. They work for newspapers, magazines, radio or television networks, Internet news services, or wire services (a news service that sends stories to multiple clients). Today's media usually rely on reports from news wire services for international news coverage rather than sending their own reporters to the scene. Only the biggest newspapers and television networks hire foreign correspondents. These reporters are usually stationed in a particular city and cover a wide territory.

Tips for Success

To be a successful foreign correspondent, you should

- have a love of adventure
- be curious about how people in other countries live
- have good interviewing skills
- have the courage to talk to people about uncomfortable topics if necessary
- have excellent communication skills
- be able to work independently
- be able to handle deadline pressure

Education and Training

You can begin to prepare for a career as a reporter or correspondent in high school. Take courses in English, writing, history, typing, foreign language, and computer science. After high school, you should go to college and earn a bachelor's degree. Your degree can be in journalism or liberal arts. Master's degrees are becoming more important for journalists, particularly for teachers and specialists.

If you plan to specialize in a particular subject, such as science or politics, it is important to take several courses in that subject. Some reporters and correspondents even earn a second degree in their specialty area.

Earnings

According to the U.S. Department of Labor, the median salary for reporters and correspondents was $34,530 in 2010. The lowest paid 10 percent of these workers earned $20,000 or less per year. The highest paid 10 percent made $75,000 or more annually. Mean annual earnings for reporters employed in newspaper, book, and directory publishing were $38,420.

Salaries for foreign correspondents depend on the publication, network, station, or other employer for which they work. Salaries range from less than $50,000 a year to an average of about $75,000 a year. The highest paid foreign correspondents earn $100,000 or more a year. Some employers pay for living expenses, such as the costs of a home, school for the correspondent's children, and a car.

News Pioneers

James Gordon Bennett Sr. (1795–1872), a U.S. journalist and publisher of the *New York Herald,* was responsible for many firsts in the newspaper industry. He was the first publisher to sell papers through newsboys. He was the first to use illustrations for news stories. He was the first to publish stock-market prices and daily financial articles. And he was the first to employ European correspondents.

Bennett's son, James Gordon Bennett Jr. (1841–1918), carried on the family business and in 1871, sent Henry M. Stanley to central Africa to find Dr. David Livingstone, a medical missionary who was missing for six years.

FOR MORE INFO

The society promotes the interests of freelance writers.

American Society of Journalists and Authors
1501 Broadway, Suite 403
New York, NY 10036-5507
212-997-0947
http://www.asja.org

To read *The Journalist's Road to Success: A Career Guide*, visit the DJNF Web site.

Dow Jones News Fund (DJNF)
PO Box 300
Princeton, NJ 08543-0300
609-452-2820
djnf@dowjones.com
https://www.newsfund.org

For information on careers, contact

National Association of Broadcasters
1771 N Street, NW
Washington, DC 20036-2800
202-429-5300
nab@nab.org
http://www.nab.org

For information on careers in newspapers and industry facts and figures, contact

Newspaper Association of America
4401 Wilson Boulevard, Suite 900
Arlington, VA 22203-1867
571-366-1000
http://www.naa.org

Visit the association's Web site for information on membership for high school and college students.

Online News Association
PO Box 65741
Washington, DC 20035-5741
646-290-7900
http://journalists.org

For a variety of journalism resources, visit the SPJ Web site.

Society of Professional Journalists (SPJ)
Eugene S. Pulliam National Journalism Center
3909 North Meridian Street
Indianapolis, IN 46208-4011
Tel: 317-927-8000
http://www.spj.org

Visit the following Web site for information on journalism careers, summer programs, and college journalism programs.

High School Journalism
http://www.hsj.org

Outlook

Employment for reporters and domestic correspondents is expected to be only fair during the next decade. In television news, budget cutbacks have affected most large stations and all of the networks. While the number of self-employed reporters is expected to grow, newspaper and magazine jobs are expected to decrease because of mergers, consolidations, and closures. Newspapers in large cities usually hire reporters with some experience, so beginning journalists will find more jobs in small towns or at smaller publications and stations. Some major daily newspapers offer a limited number of one-year, full-time internships for new reporters, with no guarantee that they will be kept on afterward.

The number of foreign correspondent jobs has declined at newspapers and magazines. It will increase if another major conflict or war (such as the Iraq War), political development, or global health outbreak or other type of disaster occurs. In the near future, most job openings will arise from the need to replace those correspondents who leave their jobs. There will also be increasing opportunities at news-oriented Web sites.

Science and Medical Writers

What Science and Medical Writers Do

Science and medical writers translate technical, medical, and scientific information so it can be easily understood by people like you and your parents, as well as professionals in the field. They research, interpret, write, and edit scientific and medical information. Their work appears in books, technical studies and reports, magazine articles, newspapers, newsletters, on Web sites. It also may be used for radio and television broadcasts.

Educational publishers hire science and medical writers to write or edit educational materials for the medical profession. Or that same publisher may hire writers to write online articles or interactive courses that are offered over the Internet.

A science or medical writer may write medical information

EXPLORING

- Take writing classes at school or at your local community center.
- Read books and magazines about science and medical topics. Your school or local librarian should be able to suggest some good titles.
- Read books about the art of writing. See the Browse and Learn More section for some suggestions.
- Write a short article for your parents or friends that explains a medical or science news story you read about online or in a newspaper or magazine.
- Ask your science or health teacher to arrange an information interview with a science or medical writer.
- Hone your writing skills by writing as much as possible.

DID YOU KNOW?

Where Science and Medical Writers Work

- Government agencies
- Insurance companies
- Medical and scientific associations
- Medical publishers
- Medical research institutions
- Newspapers and magazines
- Nonprofit organizations
- Pharmaceutical and drug companies
- Self-employment

and consumer publications about a new drug made by a pharmaceutical company. Research facilities employ them to edit reports or write about their scientific or medical studies.

Science and medical writers may work as *public information officers.* They write press releases that inform the public about the latest scientific or medical research findings. A press release is a short summary of the most important points of scientists' research findings. They are sent via e-mail or by mail to people who will share this information with others.

To be a good writer who covers subjects in detail, science and medical writers must ask a lot of questions and enjoy hunting for information that might add to the article. They do hours of research on the Internet or in libraries. Sometimes writers interview doctors, pharmacists, scientists, engineers, managers, and others who know a lot about the topic. They may have to include graphs, photos, or historical facts. If they write stories that appear on the Internet, they may shoot video, take photos, or create drawings that help people understand the story better. This type of creative work may also be done by *science and medical videographers, photographers,* or *illustrators.*

Some medical and science writers specialize in their subject matter. For instance, a medical writer may write only about heart disease and become known as the best writer on that subject. Another may focus on covering scientific developments relating to cancer. Science writers may limit their writing or focus on only one subject such as air pollution or spaceflight.

Education and Training

If you are considering a career as a writer, you should take as many English and writing classes as you can. Computer classes will also be helpful. If you know in high school that you want to do scientific or medical writing, you should take biology, physiology, chemistry, physics, math, health, and other science courses.

Not all writers go to college, but today's employers almost always require applicants to have a bachelor's degree. Many

Questions and More Questions

As a science or medical writer, you might be asked to report on a new heart surgery or other procedure that will soon be available to the public. You will need to find answers to questions like the following:

- How is the surgery performed?
- What areas of the heart (or applicable body part) are affected?
- How does a healthy heart work and how does a diseased heart work in comparison?
- How will this surgery help the patient?
- How many people are affected by this disease?
- What are the symptoms?
- How many procedures have been done successfully?
- Where were they performed?
- What is the recovery time?
- Are there are any complications?

In addition, interviews with doctors and patients will add a personal touch to your story.

FOR MORE INFO

For information on a career as a medical writer, contact
American Medical Writers Association
30 West Gude Drive, Suite 525
Rockville, MD 20850-1161
301-294-5303
amwa@amwa.org
http://www.amwa.org

For information on careers in science writing, contact
Council for the Advancement of Science Writing
PO Box 910
Hedgesville, WV 25427-0910
304-754-6786
http://www.casw.org

To read advice for beginning science writers, visit the association's Web site.
National Association of Science Writers
PO Box 7905
Berkeley, CA 94707-0905
510-647-9500
http://www.nasw.org

For information on careers in technical communication, contact
Society for Technical Communication
9401 Lee Highway, Suite 300
Fairfax, VA 22031-1803
703-522-4114
stc@stc.org
http://www.stc.org

writers earn an undergraduate degree in English, journalism, or liberal arts and then obtain a master's degree in a communications field such as medical or science writing.

Earnings

There are no specific salary studies for science and medical writers. The U.S. Department of Labor reports that all writers earned salaries that ranged from less than $29,000 to more than $109,000 in 2010. Writers who worked for newspaper, periodical, book, and directory publishers earned mean salaries of about $56,000.

Outlook

There is a lot of competition for writing jobs. Only the most talented and hardworking writers will be able to land jobs.

As we see more advances in medicine and science, there will continue to be a need for skilled writers to provide that information to the public and professionals. Those with master's degrees in medical or science writing will have the best employment prospects.

Screenwriters

EXPLORING

- One of the best ways to learn about screenwriting is to read and study scripts. Watch a movie while following the script at the same time.
- Read books about working as a screenwriter. See the Browse and Learn More section for some suggestions.
- Read industry publications. See the Browse and Learn More section for some suggestions.
- There are computer software programs that can help you create a screenplay. Check if they are available at your local or community library.
- Write a play for your classmates or friends to perform. Have a friend who is interested in film video record the performance.
- Talk to a screenwriter about his or her career.

What Screenwriters Do

A screenplay details everything that happens in a movie or television show, including dialogue, video and audio instructions, and the movements of the actors. *Screenwriters* write scripts for movies and television shows. The themes may be their own ideas or stories assigned by a producer or director. Often, screenwriters are hired to turn, or adapt, popular plays or novels into screenplays. Writers of original screenplays create their own stories, which are produced for the movie industry or television programs, such as comedies, dramas, documentaries, variety shows, and entertainment specials.

Screenwriters must not only be creative, but they must also have great research skills. For projects such as historical movies, documentaries, and medical or science programs, research is a very important step.

DID YOU KNOW?

Women screenwriters were much more prominent in the early days of filmmaking. Half of the films made before 1925 were written by women, such as Frances Marion (*Stella Dallas, The Scarlet Letter*) and Anita Loos (*The Women*). Marion was the highest-paid screenwriter from 1916 to the 1930s, and she served as the first vice president of the Writer's Guild. Though a smaller percentage of feature films written by women are produced today, more women screenwriters have won Academy Awards since 1985 than in all the previous years. Among recent Oscar winners are Ruth Prawer Jhabvala (*A Room With a View* and *Howard's End*), Jane Campion (*The Piano*), Callie Khouri (*Thelma and Louise*), Emma Thompson (*Sense and Sensibility*), Sofia Coppola *(Lost in Translation),* and Diablo Cody *(Juno).*

Screenwriters start with an outline, or a treatment, of the story's plot. Scripts are written in a two-column format. One column is used for dialogue and sound, the other for video instructions. One page of script equals about one minute of running time, though it varies. Each page has about 150 words and takes about 20 seconds to read. When the director or producer approves the story outline, screenwriters then complete the story for production. During the writing process, screenwriters write many drafts (versions) of the script. They frequently meet with directors and producers to discuss script changes.

Some screenwriters work alone and others work with a team of writers. Many specialize in certain types of scripts, such as dramas, comedies, and documentaries. *Motion picture screenwriters* usually write alone or with a writing partner and exclusively for movies. Screenwriters for television series work very long hours in the studio. Many television shows have limited runs, so much of the work for television screenwriters is not continuous.

Education and Training

In high school, you should develop your writing skills by taking English, theater, speech, and journalism classes. Social studies and foreign language classes can also be helpful in creating interesting scripts. Other important classes include history, psychology, and computer science.

A college degree is not required, but a liberal arts education is helpful because it exposes you to a wide range of subjects. Some colleges offer degrees in screenwriting or film studies. While in school, become involved in theater to learn about all of the elements required by a screenplay, such as characters, plots, and themes. Book clubs, creative writing classes, and film study are also good ways to learn the basic elements of screenwriting.

Earnings

Annual wages for screenwriters vary widely. Some screenwriters make hundreds of thousands of dollars from their scripts. Others write and film their own scripts without receiving any payment at all, relying on backers and loans. Screenwriters

The Oscar Goes To. . .

The following screenwriters were Oscar winners for best original screenplay:

- 2010: David Seidler for *The King's Speech*
- 2009: Mark Boal for *The Hurt Locker*
- 2008: Dustin Lance Black for *Milk*
- 2007: Diablo Cody for *Juno*
- 2006: Michael Arndt for *Little Miss Sunshine*

For more information on Academy Award-winning films, visit http://awardsdatabase.oscars.org.

who work independently do not earn regular salaries. They are paid a fee for each script they write. Those who write for ongoing television shows do earn regular salaries. According to the Writers Guild of America (WGA) 2008 Theatrical and Television Basic Agreement, earnings for writers of an original screenplay ranged from $62,642 to $117,602 during the 2010-11 segment of the contract. The U.S. Department of Labor reports that writers employed in the movie industry had mean annual earnings of $78,680 in 2010. Television writers earned $66,110 a year, on average.

Outlook

It will be hard to land a job as a screenwriter because so many people are attracted to the field. In this industry, it is helpful to network and make contacts. If you want to be a screenwriter, it is important to work hard to break into the field and never stop following your dreams. On the brighter side, the growth of the cable industry has increased demand for original screenplays and adaptations. Additionally, people in foreign countries are increasingly interested in watching American movies. These developments should create more demand for screenwriters.

FOR MORE INFO

To learn more about the film and television industries, to read interviews and articles by noted screenwriters, and to find links to many other screenwriting-related sites on the Internet, visit the following WGA Web sites:

Writers Guild of America (WGA)
East Chapter
250 Hudson Street
New York, NY 10013-1413
212-767-7800
http://www.wgaeast.org

Writers Guild of America (WGA)
West Chapter
7000 West Third Street
Los Angeles, CA 90048-4329
800-548-4532
http://www.wga.org

Songwriters

What Songwriters Do

Songwriters write the words and sometimes the music for songs, including songs for recordings, advertising jingles, and theatrical performances. They may also perform these songs. Songwriters who write only the words and not the music are called *lyricists*.

Songwriters may choose to write about emotions, such as love, happiness, or sadness. They put their ideas into a small number of words, focusing on the sounds of the words together. Many songwriters carry a notebook and write about things that they hear or see. Others use computers to record their thoughts. They may write songs about people, events, or experiences. They may write about broad themes that will be understood by everyone. They get ideas from current events or social situations such as poverty, racial issues, or war. Or they may write about personal issues, based on their own experiences or conversations with others.

Singer and songwriter James Taylor performs at an outdoor concert. (AP Photo/Richard Drew)

Songwriters usually have a musical style in mind when they write lyrics. These styles include pop, rock, hip hop, rap, country, blues, jazz, and classical.

Songwriters who work for advertising agencies have to write about certain products for radio and television commercials. Producers also hire songwriters to write lyrics for opera, movies, or Broadway shows. (Broadway is the name given to the main theater district in New York City.)

Many songwriters have a certain method for writing songs. Sometimes, they write the title first because it allows them to capture a theme in just a few words. The first words of the song

DID YOU KNOW?

- Francis Scott Key (1780–1843) became famous for writing the words to the "Star Spangled Banner," which was set to a popular drinking tune.
- The song "Happy Birthday to You," was written by two sisters, Mildred and Patty Hill in 1893. It was originally published under the title "Good Morning to You," but didn't become popular until the words "Good Morning" were changed to "Happy Birthday."

are often the strongest, to get the attention of the listener. Many songwriters find that there are about four common characteristics found in a song: an identifiable, universal idea; a memorable title; a strong beginning; and an appropriate form, including rhythm, verse, and refrain.

Lyricists who do not write music work with a composer. The composer might play a few measures on an instrument and the lyricist tries to write words that fit well with the music. Or, the lyricist suggests a few words or lines and the composer tries to write music that fits the words. Each partner must trust the other's talent and be able to work together to create a full song.

Education and Training

Songwriters must have a good understanding of language and grammar. In high school, you should take courses in English composition, poetry, music theory, and journalism. Learning how to play a musical instrument is a good idea. You also should take classes in musical composition.

There is really no formal training that a songwriter must have in order to write songs. Musical training is important, though. Songwriting workshops often are offered by community colleges and music schools. College music programs teach you how to read music and understand harmony. They also expose you to a variety of musical styles.

Earnings

Songwriters' earnings vary from almost nothing to many millions of dollars. A songwriter may write songs for several years before actually selling or recording a song. Songwriters receive royalties (payments) if their songs are played on the radio, in movies and on television shows, at sporting events, or in other settings. Royalties from a song may reach $20,000 per year or more for each song. A successful songwriter may earn $100,000 or more a year from the royalties of several songs.

Words to Learn

chorus a verse that is repeated throughout a song; also, a group of people singing

commission payment for a single work or a series of works

counterpoint the use of more than one melody at the same time

harmony a combination of musical notes mixed with intervals and chords

interval in music, the distance between two pitches

key a scale that provides the harmonic material for a piece of music (a piece of music that is based on the C major scale, for example, is said to be "in the key" of C major)

lyrics the words of a song

notation a written system representing musical sounds

phrasing the manner in which lyrics in a musical composition are presented by a singer

pitch the lowness or highness of a tone

refrain music or lyrics that are repeated during a song

rhythm the organized movement of a musical composition over time

scale a particular set of notes arranged in an ascending or descending order

structure the makeup of a song or musical composition

tempo Italian for speed; the speed at which a piece of music is played

timing in music, the proper spacing between various musical elements

tone a sound of a particular pitch

verse words that come before or after the chorus

Source: EssentialsofMusic.com

FOR MORE INFO

Contact these organizations to learn about the industry and opportunities available to young musicians.

American Federation of Musicians of the United States and Canada
1501 Broadway, Suite 600
New York, NY 10036-5505
212-869-1330
http://www.afm.org

American Guild of Musical Artists
1430 Broadway, 14th Floor
New York, NY 10018-3308
212-265-3687
http://www.musicalartists.org

American Society of Composers, Authors, and Publishers
One Lincoln Plaza
New York, NY 10023-7129
212-621-6000
http://www.ascap.com

To participate in online forums about music education and to read a variety of useful online brochures, such as *Careers in Music* and *How to Nail a College Entrance Audition*, visit the following Web site:

MENC: The National Association for Music Education
1806 Robert Fulton Drive
Reston, VA 20191-4341
800-336-3768
http://www.menc.org

For information on choosing a music school and a database of accredited music schools in the United States, visit the NASM Web site.

National Association of Schools of Music (NASM)
11250 Roger Bacon Drive, Suite 21
Reston, VA 20190-5248
703-437-0700
info@arts-accredit.org
http://nasm.arts-accredit.org

The society represents composers, lyricists, and songwriters who work in film, television, and multimedia. Visit its Web site for career resources, an online hall of fame, and information on *The SCORE*, its quarterly publication.

Society of Composers & Lyricists
8447 Wilshire Boulevard, Suite 401
Beverly Hills CA 90211-3209
310-281-2812
http://thescl.com

The SGA offers song critiques and workshops in select cities. Visit its Web site for more information on such events.

Songwriters Guild of America (SGA)
5120 Virginia Way, Suite C22
Brentwood, TN 37027-7594
615-742-9945
http://www.songwritersguild.com

Outlook

Songwriters find much competition in their field. It is a career much like acting, in which many people are attracted to the work. But to be a successful songwriter requires much hard work. It may take years of writing and submitting your songs to earn a reputation and become successful. On the other hand, you may be very talented, but never get that big break that allows you to have a full-time career as a songwriter. Songwriters should find more opportunities outside of the recording industry, writing music for original cable programming, multimedia projects, advertising, and the Internet.

Sportswriters

What Sportswriters Do

Sportswriters write about sports for newspapers, magazines, books, and the Internet. They research their own ideas or follow breaking stories. They interview coaches, athletes, team owners, and managers. Sometimes sportswriters write their own columns, in which they give their opinions on current news or developments in sports.

The sportswriter's main job is to report on the sports events that occur each day. In order to cover all the high school, college, and professional sports events that happen every day, sportswriters use wire news services to learn details about an event or game. Wire news services, such as Reuters, AP (Associated Press), and UPI (United Press International), gather news and make it available to many publications.

Sports events not covered by wire services are often covered by *stringers*. Stringers are reporters and writers who work part time for publications. They are paid by the number of words or lines they write. Stringers might report on high

EXPLORING

- Read books about writing. See the Browse and Learn More section for some suggestions.
- Work for your school paper as a reporter or sportswriter.
- If you can't write for school publications, then start writing about sports on your own to get experience.
- Learn all you can about different sports.
- Interview a sportswriter about his or her career.

school events, sports events in out-of-the way locations, or less popular competitions.

Sportswriters might report events that happened anywhere from a few minutes ago, to the day before, to events that took place within the week or month. *Internet sportswriters* can write about sports as they happen or as soon as a game is completed. *Newspaper sportswriters* have tighter deadlines because they have daily schedules. They may have only a few hours to conduct research and gather comments. *Magazine sportswriters* often have anywhere from several weeks to several months to

Sportswriters interview a professional baseball player. (J. Commentucci, *Syracuse Newspapers*/The Image Works)

An Award for Baseball Writers

In 1962, the J. G. Taylor Spink Award was created by the Baseball Writers' Association of America to honor a baseball writer (or other writer) "for meritorious contributions to baseball writing." J. G. Taylor Spink (1888–1962), the editor of *The Sporting News*, received the first award. Spink started out in the field as a copyboy at the *St. Louis Post-Dispatch*, but soon was hired at his father's weekly magazine, *The Sporting News*. When his father passed away, he took over operation of the paper and became a jack-of-all-trades—handling writing, editing, advertising, and publishing. He became known as "Mr. Baseball" because of his many achievements in the field and his promotion of the game as the national pastime. Each year, the award is presented at the Baseball Hall of Fame Induction Ceremony.

research and write a story. *Book sportswriters* often take years to conduct research and write detailed profiles of athletes, teams, or famous sporting events. Of course, many publications are now on the Internet. This requires sportswriters to write articles more quickly so that they can be posted online.

After sportswriters gather facts and opinions, they write the story. Most print sportswriters have to think carefully about the length of their articles. They usually have to write enough to fill a certain space. That space can change at a moment's notice, so they must be able to quickly make articles shorter or longer to

Tips for Success

To be a successful sportswriter, you should

- love sports
- have excellent writing skills
- know a lot about sports
- have good interviewing skills
- be willing to work long and non-traditional hours to cover sporting events
- have the ability to work under deadline pressure

FOR MORE INFO

The AWSM is a membership organization of women and men who work in sports writing, editing, broadcast and production, public relations, and sports information.
Association for Women in Sports Media (AWSM)
3899 North Front Street
Harrisburg, PA 17110-1583
http://awsmonline.org

To learn more about baseball writers, visit
Baseball Writers' Association of America
info@bbwaa.com
http://bbwaa.com

To read *The Journalist's Road to Success: A Career Guide*, visit the DJNF Web site.
Dow Jones News Fund (DJNF)
PO Box 300
Princeton, NJ 08543-0300
609-452-2820
djnf@dowjones.com
https://www.newsfund.org

For information on becoming a football writer, contact
Football Writers Association of America
http://www.sportswriters.net/fwaa

For information on a career as a newspaper columnist, contact

National Society of Newspaper Columnists
PO Box 411532
San Francisco, CA 94141-1532
415-488-6762
http://www.columnists.com

For information on award-winning sportswriters, visit
National Sportscasters and Sportswriters Association
PO Box 1545
Salisbury, NC 28145-1545
704-633-4275
http://www.nssafame.com

For information on writers who cover horse racing, contact
National Turf Writers Association
info@turfwriters.org
http://www.turfwriters.org

For information on careers in the newspaper industry, contact
Newspaper Association of America
4401 Wilson Boulevard, Suite 900
Arlington, VA 22203-1867
571-366-1000
http://www.naa.org

Visit the following Web site for detailed information about journalism careers:
High School Journalism
http://www.hsj.org

fit. Sportswriters for television and radio also must be able to write articles quickly to adjust to time requirements. Those who write for the Internet can write longer articles. They may also be asked to provide photographs and video to go along with their writing.

Education and Training

In school, take classes that allow you to practice your writing skills. These include journalism, grammar, English, and speech. Also, take classes that teach you how to use computers and the Internet.

A bachelor's degree is usually the minimum education required for sportswriters. Most sportswriters study journalism while in college. Many go on to study journalism at the graduate level. Competition for sports writing jobs is strong. Those with advanced education have the best chances for jobs.

Earnings

The median salary for writers was $55,420 a year in 2010, according to the U.S. Department of Labor. Writers just starting out in their careers earned less than $29,000 a year. Popular writers at large newspapers and magazines can earn more than $109,000 a year.

Outlook

Most top sportswriters at major newspapers and magazines stay in their jobs throughout their careers. This means that job openings occur as sportswriters retire, are laid off, or move into other markets. There are far more applicants for sports writing jobs than there are openings. It will continue to be difficult to land a job as a sportswriter during the next decade.

Technical Writers

What Technical Writers Do

Technical writers, also called *technical communicators,* use graphic design, page layout, and multimedia software to put scientific and technical information into language that is easy to understand by the public. They write manuals, technical reports, sales proposals, and scripts for television programs and educational films. Computer manuals are the most common types of manuals prepared by technical writers. The manuals that they prepare tell people how to install, assemble, use, or repair computer products and other equipment. These manuals can be as simple as instructions on how to use a printer or as complex as instructions on how to build a computer system.

Before technical writers begin writing, they gather as much information as possible about the subject. They read and review all available materials, including engineering drawings, reports, and journal articles. Technical writers interview people familiar with the topic, such as engineers, computer scientists, and computer programmers. Once they have gathered the necessary information, they write a first draft.

The writer gives copies of the rough draft to the *technical editor* and engineers to review. The technical editor corrects any errors in spelling, punctuation, and grammar and checks that all parts of the document are clear and easy to understand. The writer revises the rough draft based on comments from the engineers, computer scientists, programmers, and the editor. The technical editor again checks the final copy to make sure that all photos, illustrations, charts, and diagrams are properly

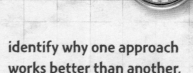

EXPLORING

- Try to gain experience in this field by working on a literary magazine, student newspaper, or yearbook.
- Read books about writing. See the Browse and Learn More section for some suggestions.
- Write in a journal daily.
- Read all sorts of books, magazines, and newspapers. This will expose you to both good and bad writing styles and techniques and help you to identify why one approach works better than another.
- Write instructions on how to use a printer or scanner for your parents or friends. Have them follow the instructions to see if you explained the steps in the right order and with the appropriate amount of detail.
- Talk to a technical writer about his or her career.

placed, that captions match the correct pictures, and that there are no other errors. The editor may ask the writer to make further revisions to the text before publication.

In addition to traditional books and paper documents, technical writers prepare materials for CD-ROMs, multimedia programs, e-publications, and Web sites.

At some companies, technical writers have other tasks. They may work as part of a team that studies a product while it is the early stages of development to make sure that it is well designed and easy to use. Others work with customer service or call center managers to help analyze and improve the quality of product support services.

DID YOU KNOW?

Approximately 48,900 technical writers are employed in the United States.

Source: U.S. Department of Labor

Education and Training

In high school, take as many English and science classes as you can. Business, journalism, math, and computer classes will also be helpful.

You will need to earn a bachelor's degree to get a job in this field. Many technical writers earn degrees in engineering or science and take technical writing classes.

Writers need to pursue learning throughout their careers to find out about new technologies, such as desktop publishing or creating multimedia programs. Experience with computer graphics and Web design will also be helpful since many writers prepare content for the Internet.

Many technical writers start their careers as computer scientists, engineers, programmers, or technicians and move into writing after a few years.

DID YOU KNOW?

Where Technical Writers Work

- Architectural, engineering, and related services companies
- Colleges and universities
- Computer and electronic manufacturing industry
- Computer systems design industry
- Management, scientific, and technical consulting services firms
- Scientific research and development services firms
- Self-employment
- Software publishers

Earnings

Median annual earnings for salaried technical writers were $63,280 in 2010, according to the U.S. Department of Labor. Earnings for technical writers ranged from less than $38,000 to more than $100,000.

Outlook

It is hard to become a writer. Each year, there are more people trying to enter this field than there are available openings. The field of technical writing, though, offers more opportunities than other areas of writing, such as journalism. Job opportuni-

FOR MORE INFO

For information on careers, contact
Association for Computing Machinery
2 Penn Plaza, Suite 701
New York, NY 10121-0701
800-342-6626
acmhelp@acm.org
http://www.acm.org

For information on computer careers
and student programs, contact
IEEE Computer Society
2001 L Street NW, Suite 700
Washington, DC 20036-4928

202-371-0101
http://www.computer.org

For information on careers in technical
communication, contact
Society for Technical Communication
9401 Lee Highway, Suite 300
Arlington, VA 22031-1803
703-522-4114
stc@stc.org
http://www.stc.org

ties for technical writers are expected to be good during the
next decade. Demand is growing for technical writers who can
produce well-written computer manuals and other technical
resources. The popularity of the Internet and the growing avail-
ability of technical materials on company Web sites will also
create more opportunities for technical writers.

Travel Writers

What Travel Writers Do

Are your parents planning your summer vacation? They might already know where they want to take you—perhaps Disney World; a visit to the museums of Washington, D.C.; or a camping trip in the mountains. But what does someone do if they don't know where they want to travel? Most often, they read articles and books about travel destinations by *travel writers.* These specialized writers are experts regarding travel destinations around the world. They know where to stay, eat, and sightsee in destinations that range from big cities and tiny towns, to state and national parks, to amusement parks, to any other places that tourists visit. They also write about cruises, train trips, and adventure travel, as well as report on developments and trends in the travel industry. Travel writers are also known as *travel authors, travel journalists, outdoor writers,* and *travel columnists.*

The work of travel writers appears in newspapers, magazines, books, and Web sites and blogs. They may also prepare marketing material for chambers of commerce, travel industry associations, and tourist bureaus. Some travel writers also appear on television and radio talk shows and documentaries.

Travel staff writers work for magazines and newspapers. They write feature articles, news stories, product reviews, and columns. They receive assignments from editors or propose their own ideas to editors. The first thing they do when writing a story is to conduct research. They do research at libraries and on the Internet, conduct phone and email interviews,

EXPLORING

- Visit http://www.natja.org to read profiles of travel writers.
- Take writing classes at school or at your local community center.
- Read books about writing. See the Browse and Learn More section for some suggestions.
- Write about a trip that you take with your parents or classmates. Write about your method of travel, where you stayed, what you ate, and what you did on your trip. Tell what you liked and disliked about the trip.
- Watch as many television shows or films about travel as possible, as well as read travel publications and visit travel Web sites.
- Talk to a travel writer about his or her career.

and, most importantly, visit the place they are writing about to gather first-hand information about the people, culture, attractions, and other aspects of the area depending on the theme of the article. They gather all the information and write it down or type it into a computer. They may also take video or photographs, which may be used to illustrate their story.

After they have gathered enough research, they create an outline that details what they will cover in the story. They submit the outline to an editor for approval. Once approved, then they begin writing the article or book. During this time, they study their research, interview more people, and continue to explore the area they are writing about. When they finish the article, they review, correct, and revise it numerous times before a final copy is submitted to an editor for further revision, fact checking, and proofreading. The editor may ask the writer to make additional changes or revise or expand the assignment as necessary.

Travel columnists analyze news and social issues as they relate to the travel industry. They write about events from the standpoint of their own experience or opinion.

Education and Training

There are many high school classes that will help prepare you for a career in writing. These include English, speech, creative writing, literature, foreign languages, history, social studies, computer science, and typing. Traveling with your family or on school trips will introduce you to different places and give you a chance to develop your writing skills.

Tips for Success

To be a successful travel writer, you should

- enjoy traveling
- be very organized
- enjoy learning about new cultures and traditions
- speak at least one foreign language
- not mind being away from home for long periods of time
- have excellent writing skills
- be able to meet deadlines
- know how to use a camera and audio- and video-recording equipment
- be willing to constantly market yourself to find work (freelance writers)

You will need at least a bachelor's degree to work as a travel writer. Many people want to become writers and having a degree will allow you to stand out from other job seekers. Many writers have a broad liberal arts background or pursue degrees in English, literature, history, philosophy, or one of the social sciences. Other employers desire communications or journalism training in college. Occasionally a master's degree in a specialized writing field may be required. If you are interested in travel writing, you might want to consider a major, or at least a minor, in a travel-related area. Travel writing associations also offer workshops and classes in travel writing.

Hot International Travel Destinations

Travel agents rate the following international destinations as the most popular for tourists:

1. London, United Kingdom
2. Rome, Italy
3. Cancún, Mexico
4. Paris, France
5. Jamaica

Source: American Society of Travel Agents

Earnings

Salaries for all writers ranged from less than $29,000 to more than $109,000 in 2010, according to the U.S. Department of Labor. Writers employed by the newspaper, book, and directory publishing industries earned mean annual salaries of about $56,000.

Many travel writers work as freelancers. Part-time freelancers may earn from $5,000 to $15,000 a year. Full-time established freelance writers may earn $75,000 or more a year.

Outlook

Employment opportunities should be good for writers during the next decade. Despite this prediction, it is hard to land a full-time job as a writer because many people want to enter this exciting field. The outlook for travel writers is even more challenging. Many people dream of writing about their travels and getting paid for it. But there are only so many positions for travel writers. Although the growth of the Internet has created more opportunities for travel writers, many of these jobs are part time and low paying.

FOR MORE INFO

For information on a career as a news-paper columnist, contact
National Society of Newspaper Columnists
PO Box 411532
San Francisco, CA 94141-1532
415-488-6762
http://www.columnists.com

For information about working as a writer and union membership, contact
National Writers Union
256 West 38th Street, Suite 703
New York, NY 10018-9807
212-254-0279
http://www.nwu.org

For industry information, contact
North American Travel Journalists Association
150 South Arroyo Parkway, 2nd Floor
Pasadena, CA 91107-4150
626-376-9754
http://www.natja.org

For information on writing contests for students in grades six through 12, contact

Outdoor Writers Association of America
615 Oak Street, Suite 201
Missoula, MT 59801-2469
406-728-7434
info@owaa.org
http://owaa.org

For information about travel writing, contact
Society of American Travel Writers
11950 West Lake Park Drive, Suite 320
Milwaukee, WI 53224-3049
414-359-1625
info@satw.org
http://www.satw.org

For information about journalism, contact
Society of Professional Journalists
Eugene S. Pulliam National Journalism Center
3909 North Meridian Street
Indianapolis, IN 46208-4011
317-927-8000
http://www.spj.org

Writers

EXPLORING

- Read books about writing. See the Browse and Learn More section for some suggestions.
- Take writing classes at school or at your local community center.
- Read all kinds of writing—fiction, nonfiction, poetry, essays. Read books, newspapers, and magazines.
- Write every day. Keep a separate notebook just for journal writing. Try not to worry about grammar, punctuation, and spelling. The important thing is to express yourself freely.
- Work as a reporter or writer on school newspapers, yearbooks, and literary magazines.
- Talk to writers about their careers.

What Writers Do

Writers express their ideas in words for books, magazines, newspapers, advertisements, radio, television, and the Internet. *Writers* are also known generally as *authors*.

Writers usually specialize in a particular type of writing. For example, those who write scripts for motion pictures or television are called *screenwriters* or *scriptwriters*. *Playwrights* do similar writing but for theater (plays). Those who write copy for advertisements are called *copywriters*.

Newswriters prepare stories for newspapers, radio, and TV. They are also called *reporters* and *correspondents*. *Columnists* specialize in writing about matters from their personal viewpoints. *Critics* review and comment upon the work of other authors, musicians, artists, and performers. Others review the quality of the food and service at restaurants.

J. K. Rowling is one of the most popular children's book authors in the world.
(National Pictures/Topham/The Image Works)

DID YOU KNOW?

Where Writers Work

- Advertising agencies
- Book publishers
- Corporations
- Film production companies
- Government agencies
- Internet companies
- Magazines
- Newspapers
- Nonprofit organizations
- Public relations firms
- Radio and television broadcasting companies
- Self-employment

Technical writers express technical and scientific ideas in easy-to-understand language. *Science and medical writers* translate technical, medical, and scientific information so it can be easily understood.

In addition to all of these types of writers, there are also *creative writers,* including *novelists, biographers, poets, essayists, comedy writers, bloggers,* and *short-story writers.*

Creative writers usually do not work on assignment, but choose their own topics and styles. Creative writers are somewhat different in this regard from journalists, copywriters, and others who are normally assigned topics by editors or publishers.

Good writers gather as much information as possible about a subject and then carefully check the accuracy of their sources. This can involve extensive library research, interviews, and long hours of observation and personal experience. Writers keep notes from which they prepare an outline or summary. They write a first draft and then rewrite sections of the material, always searching for the best way to express an idea or opinion. A manuscript is reviewed, corrected, and revised many times before a final copy is ready. *Editors* review and correct the work of writers.

Education and Training

A college education is usually necessary if you want to become a writer. You should also know how to use a computer for word processing and be able to conduct research on the Internet. Some employers prefer to hire people who have a communications or journalism degree. Others require majors in English, literature, history, philosophy, or one of the social sciences. Technical writers should have a background in engineering, business, computers, or one of the sciences. Many science and medical writers earn an undergraduate degree in English,

Fame & Fortune: Stephenie Meyer (b. 1973)

One night Stephenie Meyer dreamt of a beautiful teenage girl who met a crystal-skinned vampire. A nightmare? Hardly, since this dream sequence inspired the popular *Twilight* series for teens.

Meyer was a stay-at-home mom to three young boys at the time. She had an English degree from Brigham Young University, but no writing experience. When she awoke from the dream, Meyer immediately wrote it down—as a way to remember and analyze it later. Three months later, Meyer had transformed her notes into a story long enough to be a novel.

Meyer sent copies of her manuscript to several literary agents. Only one agreed to represent her. Meyer eventually signed a $750,000 multibook deal with Little, Brown and Company. The first book in the series, *Twilight*, hit the top of the *New York Times* Best Seller List for

Children's Books. The following installments of the vampire romance—*New Moon* (2006), *Eclipse* (2007), and *Breaking Dawn* (2008)—all landed on the *New York Times* Best Seller List. The *Twilight* books have sold more than 100 million copies worldwide. They have been translated into 37 different languages and have been adapted into a popular series of movies.

Meyer herself is surprised at the popularity of her work. She does not consider herself a good author, but rather a good storyteller. She draws upon music and classic literature as some of the inspirations for her characters and their storylines.

In 2008, Meyer was named *USA Today*'s "Author of the Year."

Sources: Answers.com, *Entertainment Weekly*, StephenieMeyer.com

FOR MORE INFO

For information on careers in medical writing, contact
American Medical Writers Association
30 West Gude Drive, Suite 525
Rockville, MD 20850-1161
301-294-5303
amwa@amwa.org
http://www.amwa.org

For information on careers in newspaper reporting, contact
American Society of Journalists and Authors
1501 Broadway, Suite 403
New York, NY 10036-5507
212-997-0947
http://www.asja.org

For information about a career as an education writer, contact
Education Writers Association
2122 P Street, NW, Suite 201
Washington, DC 20037-1037
202-452-9830
ewa@ewa.org
http://www.ewa.org

For information on careers in science writing, contact
National Association of Science Writers
PO Box 7905
Berkeley, CA 94707-0905
510-647-9500
http://www.nasw.org

This organization offers student memberships for those interested in opinion writing.

National Conference of Editorial Writers
3899 North Front Street
Harrisburg, PA 17110-1583
717-703-3015
ncew@pa-news.org
http://www.ncew.org

For information on a career as a newspaper columnist, contact
National Society of Newspaper Columnists
PO Box 411532
San Francisco, CA 94141-1532
415-488-6762
http://www.columnists.com

For information about working as a writer and union membership, contact
National Writers Union
256 West 38th Street, Suite 703
New York, NY 10018-9807
212-254-0279
nwu@nwu.org
http://www.nwu.org

For a variety of journalism resources, visit the SPJ Web site.
Society of Professional Journalists (SPJ)
Eugene S. Pulliam National Journalism Center
3909 North Meridian Street
Indianapolis, IN 46208-4011
317-927-8000
http://www.spj.org

journalism, or liberal arts and then obtain a master's degree in a communications field such as medical or science writing.

Many novelists, poets, playwrights, and short-story writers learn their skills on their own. A few become successful without a college education, but most have attended at least some college-level courses. Classes and writing groups can be found almost anywhere, from community colleges to local libraries to the Web.

Earnings

Writers earned median salaries of $55,420 in 2010, according to the U.S. Department of Labor. Beginning writers' salaries range from $20,000 to $28,000 per year. Experienced writers may earn between $38,000 and $75,000. Best-selling authors may make well over $100,000 per year, but they are few in number.

Outlook

Many people want to become writers. This makes it hard to land a full-time job in the field. The job market for creative writers is difficult to predict. Their success depends on the amount and type of work they create and their ability to sell that work. Despite the strong competition for jobs, jobs should be available at newspapers, magazines, book publishers, advertising agencies, businesses, and nonprofit organizations. Opportunities are expected to be especially good for technical writers. However, competition for jobs is very intense. Writers who are comfortable working with new media will have the best job prospects.

Writing Teachers

What Writing Teachers Do

Writing teachers teach students how to write and use proper grammar, spelling, and punctuation, as well as develop other writing skills. They teach students at all levels—from those at the elementary school level, to those in high school and college, to adults who want to try their hand at writing an essay, a short story, or even an entire book.

At the elementary school level, writing educators teach students proper grammar, spelling, sentence structure, and other writing skills. In addition to teaching English, *elementary school educators* also teach other subjects such as science and math. Teachers use a variety of aids to instruct their students. These aids include computers and Internet, textbooks, workbooks, magazines, newspapers, charts, and posters. Before and after school, teachers spend time planning classes. They grade papers, tests, and homework assignments, and prepare student reports.

At the secondary level, writing educators teach composition and other English classes. Others may teach specialized classes in journalistic writing or creative writing (poetry, essays, fiction, plays, etc.). In addition to classroom instruction, they plan lessons, prepare tests, grade papers, complete report cards, meet with parents, and supervise other activities. They often meet individually with students to discuss homework assignments or academic or personal problems.

College writing educators teach English and creative writing classes at two- and four-year colleges and universities. They may

EXPLORING

- Visit http://www.aft.org/pdfs/ tools4teachers/becominga teacher0608.pdf to learn more about becoming a teacher.
- Read books about writing. See the Browse and Learn More section for some suggestions.
- Teach your younger brothers or sisters about proper grammar, punctuation, and spelling.
- Talk to your teachers about their careers and their college experiences.

- Volunteer with a community center, day care center, or summer camp to get teaching experience.
- Look at course catalogs and read about the faculty members and the courses they teach. These are available at your library and on the Internet at a college's Web site.

teach entry-level courses in grammar and composition to freshman students or advanced creative writing classes to upper-level students. Many creative writing classes use the workshop approach. Students are required to write poems, essays, and short stories, which are then discussed by other students and the teacher during class. The teacher offers constructive criticism and suggestions on how the work could be improved. This helps the student become a better writer. Writing teachers also assign readings to students and lead in-class activities that help them develop their creativity and writing skills. College writing teachers may spend only 12 to 16 hours a week in the classroom, but they spend many hours preparing lectures and lesson plans, grading writing assignments and exams, and preparing grade reports. They also meet with students individually outside

*A teacher details a writing assignment for students. (Edward Pikulski, AP Photo/*The Scranton Times)

of the classroom to guide them in the course, and keep them updated about their progress.

Education and Training

During your middle- and high-school years, you should concentrate on a college preparatory program and focus on taking as many English, speech, and writing courses as possible. Many writing teachers have undergraduate degrees in English, creative writing, journalism, or a related field. They typically go on to earn graduate degrees in fine arts, journalism, or related

Helping Hands: The Hearst Journalism Awards Program

The Hearst Journalism Awards Program was established by the William Randolph Hearst Foundation, whose namesake was an American newspaper and magazine publishing mogul. Its purpose is to award monetary prizes to help support and encourage journalism students at the college level. More than $550,000 is awarded annually through monthly competitions in writing, photojournalism, broadcasting (both radio and television), and multimedia. Monthly winners for writing, photojournalism, and broadcasting are eligible to compete for championship and additional scholarships.

Earning a Hearst Journalism Award not only benefits the winning student, but also the school in which they attend—students win scholarships for themselves and matching grants for their schools.

Entrants must be actively involved in campus media, either through publication or newscast production. Students must also be enrolled in a journalism program that is accredited by the Accrediting Council on Education in Journalism and Mass Communications. Visit http://www.hearstfdn.org/hearst_journalism/about.php for more information.

Source: Hearst Journalism Awards Program

DID YOU KNOW?

Writing programs have become popular on college campuses. The number of college creative writing programs grew from 79 in 1975 to 822 in 2009, according to the Association of Writers and Writing Programs.

fields. When you enter a master's program, you will probably be required to take on some assistant-teaching responsibilities.

To teach in a four-year college or university, you must have at least a master's degree. With a master's degree you can become an instructor. You will need a doctorate for a job as an assistant professor, which is the entry-level job title for college faculty. Faculty members usually spend no more than six years as assistant professors. During this time, the college will decide whether to grant you tenure, which is a type of job security, and promote you to associate professor. An associate professor may eventually be promoted to full professor.

Earnings

According to the U.S. Department of Labor, salaries for elementary school teachers ranged from less than $35,000 to $80,000 or more annually in 2010. The median salary for secondary school teachers was $53,230. Those just starting out in the field earned less than $36,000. Very experienced teachers earned more than $83,000. College English language and literature teachers earned an average salary of $60,400 a year. Earnings ranged from less than $33,000 to $113,000 or more.

Outlook

The number of creative writing programs at colleges and universities continues to grow. There will be good employment opportunities for writing educators with strong teaching skills and a strong record of publishing success. Despite this prediction, it will be difficult for even the most qualified teachers to

FOR MORE INFO

To read about the issues affecting college professors, contact
American Association of University Professors
1133 19th Street, NW, Suite 200
Washington, DC 20036-3655
202-737-5900
http://www.aaup.org

For more information on a teaching career, contact
American Federation of Teachers
555 New Jersey Avenue, NW
Washington, DC 20001-2029
202-879-4400
http://www.aft.org

For information about college writing programs, contact
Association of Writers and Writing Programs
George Mason University
MS 1E3
Fairfax, VA 22030-4444
http://www.awpwriter.org

For information on education careers, contact
National Education Association
1201 16th Street, NW
Washington, DC 20036-3290
202-833-4000
http://www.nea.org

land jobs at top writing programs. More opportunities will be available at elementary, middle, and high schools, as well as teaching writing courses at community centers.

Glossary

accredited   approved as meeting established standards for providing good training and education; this approval is usually given by an independent organization of professionals

annual salary   the money an individual earns for an entire year of work

apprentice   a person who is learning a trade by working under the supervision of a skilled worker; apprentices often receive classroom instruction in addition to their supervised practical experience

associate's degree   an academic rank or title granted by a community or junior college or similar institution to graduates of a two-year program of education beyond high school

bachelor's degree   an academic rank or title given to a person who has completed a four-year program of study at a college or university; also called an **undergraduate degree** or **baccalaureate**

bonus   an award of money in addition to one's typical salary that is given to an employee for extra-special work or achievement on the job

career   an occupation for which a worker receives training and has an opportunity for advancement

certified   approved as meeting established requirements for skill, knowledge, and experience in a particular field; people are certified by an organization of professionals in their field

college   a higher education institution that is above the high school level

community college   a public or private two-year college attended by students who do not usually live at the college; graduates of a community college receive an associate's degree and may transfer to a four-year college or university to complete a bachelor's degree

diploma   a certificate or document given by a school to show that a person has completed a course or has graduated from the school

distance education   a type of educational program that allows students to take classes and complete their education by mail or the Internet

doctorate   the highest academic rank or title granted by a graduate school to a person who has completed a two- to three-year program after having received a master's degree

fellowship   a financial award given for research projects or dissertation assistance; fellowships are commonly offered at the graduate, postgraduate, or doctoral levels

freelancer   a worker who is not a regular employee of a company; they work for themselves and do not receive a regular paycheck

fringe benefit   a payment or benefit to an employee in addition to regular wages or salary; examples of fringe benefits include a pension, a paid vacation, and health or life insurance

graduate school   a school that people may attend after they have received their bachelor's degree; people who complete an educational program at a graduate school earn a master's degree or a doctorate

intern   an advanced student (usually one with at least some college training) in a professional field who is employed in a job that is intended to provide supervised practical experience for the student

internship   1. the position or job of an intern; 2. the period of time when a person is an intern

junior college   a two-year college that offers courses like those in the first half of a four-year college program; graduates of a junior college usually receive an associate's degree and may transfer to a four-year college or university to complete a bachelor's degree

liberal arts   the subjects covered by college courses that develop broad general knowledge rather than specific occupational skills; the liberal arts are often considered to include philosophy, literature and the arts, history, language, and some courses in the social sciences and natural sciences

major (in college)   the academic field in which a student specializes and receives a degree

master's degree   an academic rank or title granted by a graduate school to a person who has completed a one- or two-year program after having received a bachelor's degree

pension   an amount of money paid regularly by an employer to a former employee after he or she retires from working

scholarship   a gift of money to a student to help the student pay for further education

social studies   courses of study (such as civics, geography, and history) that deal with how human societies work

starting salary   salary paid to a newly hired employee; the starting salary is usually a smaller amount than is paid to a more experienced worker

technical college   a private or public college offering two- or four-year programs in technical subjects; technical colleges offer courses in both general and technical subjects and award associate's degrees and bachelor's degrees

undergraduate   a student at a college or university who has not yet received a degree

undergraduate degree   see **bachelor's degree**

union   an organization whose members are workers in a particular industry or company; the union works to gain better wages, benefits, and working conditions for its members; also called a **labor union** or **trade union**

vocational school   a public or private school that offers training in one or more skills or trades

wage   money that is paid in return for work done, especially money paid on the basis of the number of hours or days worked

Browse and Learn More

Books

Berman, Len, and Kent Gamble. *And Nobody Got Hurt!: The World's Weirdest, Wackiest True Sports Stories.* New York: Little, Brown Young Readers, 2005.

Buckley, Annie. *Movies.* Ann Arbor, Mich.: Cherry Lake Publishing, 2008.

Buckley, Annie, and Kathleen Coyle. *Once Upon a Time: Creative Writing Fun for Kids.* San Francisco: Chronicle Books, 2004.

Bull, Andy. *The NCTJ Essential Guide to Careers in Journalism.* Thousand Oaks, Calif.: Sage Publications Ltd., 2007.

Claybourne, Anna, Gillian Doherty, and Rebecca Treays. *The Usborne Encyclopedia of Planet Earth.* Tulsa, Okla.: Usborne Publishing, 2009.

Crutcher, Chris. *Athletic Shorts: Six Short Stories.* New York: HarperTempest, 2002.

Daynes, Katie, Lesley Sims, and Nilesh Mistry. *The Fabulous Story of Fashion.* Atlanta, Ga.: Usborne Books, 2006.

Diehl, David. *Sports A to Z.* Asheville, N.C.: Lark Books, 2007.

DiPrince, Dawn, and Cheryl Miller Thurston. *Unjournaling: Daily Writing Exercises that Are NOT Personal, NOT Introspective, NOT Boring!* Fort Collins, Colo.: Cottonwood Press Inc., 2006.

Dunkleberger, Amy. *So You Want to Be a Film or TV Screenwriter?* Berkeley Heights, N.J.: Enslow Publishers, 2007.

Editors of *Time for Kids* Magazine. *Time for Kids Ready, Set, Write!: A Writer's Handbook for School and Home.* New York: Time For Kids, 2006.

Fine, Janet. *Opportunities in Teaching Careers.* New York: McGraw-Hill, 2005.

Frederick, Robin. *Shortcuts to Hit Songwriting: 126 Proven Techniques for Writing Songs That Sell.* Calabasas, Calif.: Taxi Music Books, 2008.

Frings, Gini Stephens. *Fashion: From Concept to Consumer.* 9th ed. Upper Saddle River, N.J.: Prentice Hall, 2007.

Goldberg, Jan. *Careers in Journalism.* 3d ed. New York: McGraw-Hill, 2005.

Hamlett, Christina. *Screenwriting for Teens: The 100 Principles of Screenwriting Every Budding Writer Must Know.* Studio City, Calif.: Michael Wiese Productions, 2006.

Harrower, Tim. *Inside Reporting: A Practical Guide to the Craft of Journalism.* New York: McGraw-Hill Humanities/Social Sciences/Languages, 2006.

Holtz, Martina. *Voggy's ABC of Music: Basic Music Theory for Kids.* Wachtberg-Villip, Germany: Voggenreiter, 2005.

Luboff, Pete, and Pat Luboff. *101 Songwriting Wrongs and How to Right Them.* 2d ed. Cincinnati, Ohio: Writers Digest Books, 2007.

Newcomb, Rain, and Veronika Gunter. *Write Now!: The Ultimate, Grab-a-Pen, Get-the-Words-Right, Have-a-Blast Writing Book.* Asheville, N.C.: Lark Books, 2005.

Olien, Rebecca, and Michael Kline. *Kids Write!: Fantasy & Sci Fi, Mystery, Autobiography, Adventure & More!* Nashville, Tenn.: Williamson Books, 2005.

Rhatigan, Joe. *In Print!: 40 Cool Publishing Projects for Kids.* Asheville, N.C.: Lark Books, 2004.

Seskin, Steve, Eve Aldridge, Shino Arihara, Bob Barner, et al. *Sing My Song: A Kid's Guide to Songwriting.* New York: Tricycle Press, 2008.

Skog, Jason. *Screenwriting; A Practical Guide to Pursuing the Art.* Mankato, Minn.: Compass Point Books, 2010.

Smith Jr., Charles R. *Winning Words: Sports Stories and Photographs.* Somerville, Mass.: Candlewick Press, 2008.

Stalder, Erika. *Fashion 101: A Crash Course in Clothing.* San Francisco: Orange Avenue Publishing, 2008.

Streisel, Jim. *High School Journalism: A Practical Guide.* Jefferson, N.C.: McFarland & Company Inc., Publishers, 2007.

Venolia, Jan. *Kids Write Right!: What You Need to Be a Writing Powerhouse.* New York: Tricycle Press, 2004.

Periodicals

Cricket
http://www.cricketmag.com

Editor & Publisher
http://www.editorandpublisher.com

The Hollywood Reporter
http://www.hollywoodreporter.com

Plays
http://playsmagazine.com

Presstime
http://www.naa.org/Resources/Publications/PRESSTIME.aspx

Quick Hits
http://www.ire.org/quickhits

The SCORE
http://www.thescl.com/the_score

Sports Illustrated Kids
http://www.sikids.com

Time for Kids
http://www.timeforkids.com/TFK

Variety
http://www.variety.com

Writer's Digest
http://www.writersdigest.com

Web Sites

About.com: Environmental Issues
http://environment.about.com/mbody.htm

Academy of Motion Picture Arts and Sciences
http://www.oscars.org

AMC Filmsite
http://www.filmsite.org

American Amateur Press Association
http://www.aapainfo.org

American Federation of Teachers: Becoming a Teacher
http://www.aft.org/pdfs/tools4teachers/becomingateacher0608.pdf

American Film Institute
http://www.afi.com

American Library Association: Great Web Sites for Kids
http://www.ala.org/greatsites

Bartleby.com: Great Books Online
http://www.bartleby.com

Beverly Cleary
http://www.beverlycleary.com

DogEared
http://kidsblogs.nationalgeographic.com/dogeared

Fashion-Era
http://www.fashion-era.com

Food Network
http://www.foodnetwork.com

Genna's World
http://www.gennasworld.com

High School Journalism
http://www.hsj.org

The Internet Movie Database
http://www.imdb.com

JournalismJobs.com
http://www.journalismjobs.com

The Journalist's Road to Success: A Career Guide
https://www.newsfund.org

McCormick Freedom Museum
http://www.mccormickfoundation.org/Civics/programs

National Academy of Television Arts & Sciences
http://www.emmyonline.tv

Newseum
http://www.newseum.org

NewsLink
http://newslink.org

Newspapers.com
http://www.newspapers.com

The Pulitzer Prizes
http://www.pulitzer.org

ReadKiddoRead.com
http://www.readkiddoread.com/home

Read Print Publishing
http://www.readprint.com

RoaldDahl.com
http://www.roalddahl.com

Scholastic Art & Writing Awards
http://www.artandwriting.org

Scholastic: Write It
http://teacher.scholastic.com/writeit

Scholastic: Writing With Scientists
http://teacher.scholastic.com/activities/sciencewriting

Scholastic: Writing With Writers
http://teacher.scholastic.com/writewit

Shakespeare for Kids
http://www.folger.edu/template.cfm?cid=588

ShelSilverstein.com
http://www.shelsilverstein.com

Storynory
http://storynory.com

Yahoo!: Kids: Sports
http://kids.yahoo.com/sports

Yahoo!: Sports
http://sports.yahoo.com

Young Adult Books Central
http://www.yabookscentral.com

Index